PAIN IN THE ASSET MANAGER

IMPROVE PERFORMANCE THROUGH OPPORTUNISTIC GAINS

TIM NICHOLS

with Jonathan Gilstrap

A PINNACLE PROPERTY GROUP PUBLICATION

ISBN: **978-0692618158**

For my kids, who are the inspiration behind the

HATS Matrix and much of what I do...

TABLE OF CONTENTS

ACKNOWLEDGMENTS

I want to thank all of the valued friends and clients who helped shape the initial survey that ultimately led to the information provided in this book. Additionally, there are numerous clients, prospects and acquaintances who agreed to participate in the survey. The information provided by each and every person helped guide the finished work.

I am grateful for a mentor and wise friend, John T. Cocoris, for his guidance and counsel during the process. We have spent hours in conversations about this work and many others. Phillip Moss is a true friend who introduced the two of us. Without this connection, I would not be where I am today. Phillip also introduced me to Dr. George B. Burriss, who got me headed down a different path many years ago. I also want to thank T.K. Kieran, who was instrumental in pulling this concept out of the imaginary and into reality. I want to thank Jonathan Gilstrap, whose input and contributions were so valuable that he is co-author of the book. Without all of their guidance, this book would still be an idea.

I appreciate the incredible efforts of Ty and Cindy Walsworth for their creative guidance, design and clarity in editing and designing the book inside and out.

Finally, I want to thank my wife, who helped create the HATS (kids, not the Matrix), makes me efficient and is a direct inspiration of about 80% of the good things I do... using only 20% of her effort. Thanks for not wasting our time, dear!

INTRODUCTION

Congratulations! The fact that you have opened this book says you are open to learning. People that don't think they have anything to learn don't read very often. Of course, learning something new or even learning to look at the same old stuff in a different way isn't difficult. But translating that into improvement of the bottom line can be extremely difficult. Throughout this book I will challenge you to do just that.

Pain in the Asset Manager got its wings in the midst of hundreds of hours of questioning and interviewing various people involved in commercial real estate asset management. The professional career range of people interviewed varied from assistant all the way up to chairman/owner. There were hundreds of questions asked to assistants, analysts, managers, asset managers, vice presidents, directors, controllers, chief financial officers and various partners, owners, chairmen, investors, etc. We live, work and invest primarily in Texas; therefore, the vast majority of people interviewed own Texas real estate.

The range of portfolios for those interviewed began at about $5 million and went up into multiple billions, with the average portfolio of an interviewee at roughly $200 million. There was not a lot of distinction made on our end as to asset types; therefore, the assets owned by the interviewees run the full gamut of commercial real estate classes. For clarity's sake, the highest percentage of real estate assets of those interviewed was with multi-family, followed by retail, office, industrial, and finally, hospitality. Other classifications were also included but make up a significantly smaller number than those specified.

The physical location of the interviewee's corporate offices was really not important to us. Because of this, the participants in the interviews and surveys ranged coast-to-coast (with an insignificant number located internationally). This is by no means a scientifically perfect set of data, but the sample set was diverse enough that we feel it is a representative cross-section of real estate owners. For those of you who want perfect information, keep looking; however, if you are interested in taking our research and applying it to your day-to-day workload, I am certain that you will find the information and suggestions extremely valuable to you and your company.

We know asset managers have a lot of responsibilities. Furthermore, we know there are a lot of tasks that don't fall within the four walls of Asset Management, but nonetheless wind up on an asset manager's desk. We hypothesized that within this assortment of tasks there resides a select handful that have a significantly greater impact on asset performance than the rest. We conducted our research to test this hypothesis and, if validated, to also collect the very best practices in the marketplace for addressing these tasks. Our belief on the front end is that we could identify this small handful and the corresponding best practices in the marketplace. We also felt that publishing these best practices would provide valuable information to people who read it and lead to great results for those who implemented them.

A goal of this book is to make you a better and more effective asset manager. Another goal is to make this task easier than it would initially seem. I realize that this could be a tall order because I am not a good asset manager. I am not even a mediocre or bad asset manager. I am not an asset manager at all. However, I am a good listener, and I am a good compiler of data. Hopefully, these skills of mine and your great skills in your profession, combined with your ability to implement a few key things, will produce valuable results for you. If not, feel free to call me. This will be your chance to let me know where I missed the mark, as a second revision of this book is currently forthcoming. You have no idea how helpful your criticism might be!

I guess it would help to learn a little bit about me. I'm one of those shortcut experts. If there is a way to shave 15 minutes off a task, I am generally the one to find it. I guess you could say I'm somewhat of a self-proclaimed efficiency expert. I don't like to waste a lot of time. I am by no means the smartest guy in the world, but there is a creative side of me that seeks out and finds efficiency in many situations. The goal of this book was to find efficiencies in the field of commercial real estate asset management.

A lot of my philosophy on life, and hence the philosophy of this book, revolves around the Pareto Principle or the 80/20 rule. This will be discussed in a later chapter in greater detail, but the overall driving force of this book is simple: Spend your time on the things that matter most. Many of us like to think we do this on a pretty consistent basis. But we are often distracted with the things that are easy, urgent, in front of us, interesting, demanding or important to someone else. This strategy may keep our attention, keep our focus or keep us busy, but it will never ensure our effectiveness or efficiency.

As we progress through our careers and become more experienced, we also become more entrenched. For this reason, it is critical to professional performance to often step back and take an objective look at the way we function. This is difficult to do in the "hurry up and get it done" professional environment that the modern workplace has become. This short-fuse environment coupled with our modern ability to access tons of information instantly has made us more quick and information-focused and simultaneously less methodical and action oriented.

For many of us, if we were told that it was important to take a nap, we would Google nap-taking, read a few articles on it, create a spreadsheet with graphs on napping statistics, and outline a lecture on the benefits of rest. We would accomplish all of this and be able to offer a stellar presentation on resting principles, while not benefitting at all from an ounce of rest. We have mastered the art of processing information without allowing it to affect or assist us much at all. In the coming chapters, you will be presented with some new ideas, then challenged to actually implement them for the sake of your own benefit.

My personal desire to increase efficiency and effectiveness in both my personal life and professional career has often gotten me to a point of intense searching for great opportunities to save time and energy. Oftentimes, as I am looking the hardest for a solution to a given problem, the best answer comes up and taps me on the shoulder from a direction that I was never looking. I remember a story about an 18-wheeler getting stuck under an overpass. It was too tall for the stated clearance and became wedged in between the concrete sections above and below it. The best teams of "experts" racked their brains on how to get the truck loose. The experts and industry professionals were perplexed. The best heads assembled could not figure out a way to free the rig without significant additional damage to the structure and vehicle. It was a little girl who finally came along and suggested that they let some of the air out of the tires. This lowered the truck. Problem solved. No further damage. Perhaps you are looking at your career and wondering what you can do to make it better. If this is the case, I hope this book proves to be valuable to you.

Pain in the Asset Manager will walk you through certain things that have to do with real estate asset management. Some of them are going to be extremely basic and obvious, such as defining some of the roles that a real estate asset manager performs. Some of the chapters may not be so obvious or even seemingly relevant to asset management. You might think some of it is completely irrelevant to your professional style or asset management as a whole. If you get to this point, I would encourage you to take more of a holistic approach to your life and work. These outside ideas could provide great benefits to you in many areas.

Some particular content that might seem odd to you could be The Challenge brought up in Chapter 3. This is where I would encourage you to put your analytical side on hold. The creative concepts listed in this chapter may be the very things that set you apart from your peers within your company or industry as a whole. Remember these are not all my original ideas. They are the results of interviewing numerous professionals within your industry. Let me restate that: They are the *good* results of interviewing numerous professionals within your industry.

A fundamental exercise in this book is categorizing the different roles and responsibilities of an asset manager. We place these roles and responsibilities in a matrix expressing the correlation between two of our most precious and limited resources: money and time. None of these roles and responsibilities are going to be innovative in your mind; however, the categorization of them based on frequency and return could be. As we delve into this, we hope it will encourage you to divide and/or allocate your time in a more efficient and thoughtful manner. Ideally, the presentation of these different roles within this Matrix will be easy for you to remember. It simply plots roles that you already are responsible for in a manner that you may have never considered. Obviously, no one can prioritize your day better than you can. The goal of this Matrix is to enable you to assess your own priorities and determine what needs to be done by you personally and what needs to be delegated to others.

At the conclusion of this book there is a call to action. If your goal is simply to read this book, critique it and not implement any suggestions, then do yourself a favor and go ahead and set the book down. I would not want you to invest one more second in something that is not ultimately going to be to your benefit. But please do not dismiss this work saying, "I've tried everything!" Don't be like the fat person trying to lose weight who says, "Yeah! I've tried everything too!" "Have you eaten gorilla meat? I hear that it is really high in protein!" If you haven't tried that, you haven't tried everything. So as you go through this book, please try to keep an open mind. Perhaps *Pain in the Asset Manager* could be the catalyst that takes you from Asset Manager to Director of Asset Management.

CHAPTER ONE

REAL ESTATE ASSET MANAGEMENT

It's hurricane season! Storms are brewing out at sea. The calm, mild spring and summer we have experienced is coming to an end. No one knows when the storms will hit. No one knows where the storms will hit. Some could be mild and not cause problems. Others might be severe and plow into a community near you. One thing is for certain and that is uncertainty.

Let's face it, the last few years have been great for real estate in many markets for most property types. New development has been steady, and new products have performed well. In many ways, asset managers have required little more than a pulse to show adequate performance. Most would agree that this trend is starting to change. Cautious optimism is the new norm, which is another way of saying we have reasonable fears. Indicators are starting to point to a slow-down in the aggressive growth we have been experiencing recently. This will make the job of asset managers a little tougher in the coming years.

Given these indicators, we reached out and asked the market — your colleagues — to describe a good asset manager versus a poor asset manager. We were looking for roles that needed to be filled to ensure success in the position. There were two responses that seemed to repeat themselves and defined the top objectives for an asset manager. They are to:

1. Maximize return to investor, and
2. Maximize property value.

Another key ingredient that came from this line of questions is that it's critical for an asset manager to maintain a strong network of professional relationships. Being well-connected is critical to many aspects of asset management.

These responses are what led to having a mission statement for the book and shaped the way the goal or mission statement is currently written. To summarize, a good asset manager should: **Maximize Investor Returns and Property Values through a strong network of real estate professionals.**

So as we move through the book, we will discuss the various topics, strategies and practices in terms of how they contribute to one or more of the following:

1. Maximize return to investor,
2. Maximize property value, and/or
3. Strengthen relationships.

I believe it is a great idea when mapping out a plan that you have a course of direction determined for where you would like to go. Of course, the word mapping stems from the word map. One of my favorite movies is *The Count of Monte Cristo*. In it, an old man holds onto a treasure map which he gives to someone he befriends in prison. Ultimately, this map is used to locate a crazy amount of gold that you couldn't spend in three lifetimes. The map was a plan that had a goal in mind. That goal was to lay out a course of direction that anyone could follow and come to a destination where a hidden treasure could be found. For the sake of making this read more interesting, let's assume this book is a map, and there is something of great value that it will help you find. In order to do this, we have to have a goal.

I am sure everyone has heard the concept of SMART goals. There's a lot of noise in the marketplace evaluating whether or not SMART goals are of value. I came across one article entitled, *"Are SMART Goals Dumb?"* (www.leadershipiq.com/blogs/leadershipiq/35353793-are-smart-goals-dumb). It argued the point that setting a goal might actually cause people to sandbag and lower their expectations so as not to fail. I like to look at it from the other direction. If I set a very lofty goal and have 75% success, am I better off? I would say so! Others may argue this is failure. My experience says if I do not put my eye on a target, I do not come anywhere close to moving in the desired direction. But if I have a well thought out goal, I have a measurable percentage of success in the direction of the desired target. This creates a result that can be evaluated.

To review what you might already know, a SMART goal is defined as one that is: *Specific, Measurable, Achievable, Results-focused* and *Time-bound*. All of these are important criteria for heading in a new direction. Let's take a quick look at each of these and how they can contribute to your overall success.

Specific

"I want to do better." This is very vague. "I want to become a better asset manager." This is a wee bit more specific. "I want to become a better asset manager with my current company and receive a promotion to vice president of asset management." You can see the difference in the level of detail. People that set vague goals tend to get vague results. I find vague goals to be a rather poor strategy for improvement, whereas specific ones tend to chart a course of direction that is often followed.

Measurable

Poor performers tend to hate this aspect of the SMART goal. Why do they hate it? They hate "measurable" because it sets an expectation on their future performance. I have found through the years that supervisors don't necessarily care that you hit your goals as much as they see that you don't have a fear in setting them. Most of us know that people with specific intent behind their actions directed at some stated goal are going to achieve more than somebody that is simply trying really hard. This measurability component tends to value your effectiveness over your actions. The promotion to VP listed above is measurable.

Achievable

This component is where a lot of the criticism of SMART goals enters the picture. How do we really know what is achievable until we actually walk it out? The truth is, we don't. So we must develop goals that both stretch our current capacity, yet also take a realistic view of the overall effects that this goal can have. I think a good word for this is reasonable. An unrealistic goal will eventually be highly *UN-motivating* once it is determined how far off the mark someone is in achieving it.

Results-Focused

A results-focused goal simply measures the outcome and not the activity. The activities are the strategies that get you to the goal. The goal is where you end up. Some people are very forward thinking, and they like to camp out here. They enjoy talking about future concepts and ideas, but do not like delivering them. If you are one of these types, remember many of those that you work with and for don't want to hear about what you're going to do. Where you are heading is great, as long as you can back it up with how you're getting there along the way.

Time-Bound

Goals should be linked to a timeframe that creates a practical sense of urgency; this creates tension between where we are versus where we want to be. Without such tension, most of us would be quite happy focusing our efforts and attention to things that come naturally for us. This ongoing tension is the fuel that feeds activities, which will bring about the desired changes.

So with a cursory review of SMART goals, I propose the following goal while reading this book: I desire to improve myself by becoming a better asset manager in the way I maximize returns to investors and maximize property values, by improving my network of professional contacts and the way I interact with them, and to increase ROI and property values by at least 10% in the coming year. Or perhaps your SMART goal may be: In the next year, I want to become a better asset manager to advance my company and career by maximizing returns to current investors and improving property values with my expanding network of professional contacts to grow my current asset values by 10%.

Okay, those surely are a mouthful! However, they are based on responses from numerous people interviewed in all aspects of asset management. Again, I don't think of it as all-inclusive. Feel free to tweak it along the way to match your personal desires. Just remember to eliminate ambiguity and uncertainty. If it is true that the landscape of asset managers will undergo some changes in the coming months and years, then it is important for those who plan to stay ahead of the pack to start making some specific plans.

The goal that is listed above may not be yours exactly, but until you elaborate and articulate yours, just use mine for the time being. It will serve your needs for guiding you through this simple read.

Returns and Value

The initial point of this chapter was to identify how to be a better real estate asset manager. Of course, that is really the point of this entire book. Let's start with the survey question that we asked participants:

> ***Help define a good asset manager versus a poor asset manager. What metrics does your firm use to evaluate this?***

Before identifying all of the little "Returns on Whatever" that different companies use, recall the two core objectives already mentioned: Maximize Return to the Investor and

Maximize Property Value. Obviously, these are both important in the role of asset management.

These two objectives seem to be pretty obvious, but they will not always play themselves out in the same way. Depending on investment strategy, returns to investors might be realized as monthly revenue or a one-time distribution at the sale of the property. In the same way, maximizing property value could be in the quick value-add or long-term play. It is beyond the scope of this book to dissect every little nuance to determine maximizing investor return on different types of assets. As we stated earlier, nobody knows how to plan out your day-to-day activities better than you do. And no one knows the objectives of your company better than you. Our goal is to deliver universal tangibles for all asset classes, regardless of your investment objectives.

Also, as we go through and learn about maximizing returns and property values, we're probably not going to shed tons of new light on how to make great gains in *all* the areas that we cover. However, since they are such an integral part in the role of asset management, we at least need to pay them lip service. Further, there are numerous ideas that we came across that you can implement that have a measurable impact. But most of these are not part of the forthcoming Big Three, a key component of the Grand Slam of Asset Management detailed in Chapters 3 and 10.

When it comes to maximizing returns and property values, let's start by stating the obvious: You can do one without doing the other. For instance, if your only objective was to maximize the return of the investors, you could easily dismantle every piece of the asset and sell it for scrap value. However, eventually you would have no property value as everything would be liquidated. On the other side of the equation, you could also maximize property value by spending all of the incoming money on platinum and solid gold fixtures. This would leave little, if any, left over for the investors. So let's separate the two and give each a cursory discussion.

Maximize Return to Investors

Maximizing return to investors through cash flow can be achieved by increasing revenue and/or decreasing expenses. During our research, we came across a number of suggestions on how to achieve increased returns by implementing both sides of this equation. Along the same lines, there is also a way to increase intangibles, such as goodwill. Increasing goodwill or other intangibles can create a long-term effect that gives both a higher return to the investor and also increases property value.

Increase Revenue

Obviously revenues can increase by market-driven factors. Since we have no control over those, it is really not within our scope to discuss how to ride this wave or avoid it. So when we talk about increasing revenues, we are discussing additional sources of revenue, not how to increase rent or tenancy.

Rooftop Revenue

There are a few ways to monetize the rooftop of a structure. One of the most interesting that I came across was renting the roof space out to utility companies to produce solar panel farms for generation of electricity. This application makes the most sense for industrial properties where the square footage is spread out versus stacked. This seems to be a relatively new concept, and I would not say all of the kinks are worked out of this yet. One of the major concerns seems to be the cost of removing the panels when the roof structure underneath needed to be replaced. Once the possible kinks are worked out, this could be a nice source of revenue for many landlords who want to take advantage of this as an additional stream of income.

Perhaps a good business to embark on is a device that would allow roof solar panels to be attached securely to the structure while simultaneously being easy to remove, therefore installation and removal does not cause a penetration to the roof itself. I'm not sure how you would solve this problem, but I bet there's a future for the person who figures it out.

Antenna/Cell Tower

A not-so-new concept is renting rooftop space on taller buildings to cell phone companies or broadcasters for cell towers or antennas. These may not be the greatest opportunities to try to seek out; because it seems that if you were a viable candidate, an interested party would have reached out to you. However, exploration in this area could produce an additional stream of revenue for minimal investment.

Parking Revenue

Depending on the type of asset, parking can be an additional source of revenue. It is not likely going to have a significant impact on ROI, but it is certainly worth evaluating. From reserved parking to garage parking, close parking, covered parking, and even event parking, there are always people willing to pay a little bit more for special treatment. My wife would gladly pay 5 to 10 bucks at the cash register for a front row spot at the grocery store.

Advertising Revenue

Advertising revenue can come in a lot of different forms. It is not specific to any single asset class and is an arena where creativity can likely have some impact. There are a number of different businesses who would like to target your tenants and their customers. The good thing about advertising revenue is that it is relatively painless to manage. The right mix, once set in motion, can be quite easy to oversee. If you have a periodic tenant newsletter or other form of contact, think of all of the advertisers in the area who might be willing to "sponsor" this by offering ad space.

Creative Operating Expenses

I thought this one was pretty interesting. This would likely only work in a multitenant office or retail environment, but I thought it was still worth a mention. Also, no one is going to retire off of this idea, but it goes in the section of "every little bit helps." A national office REIT based out of Georgia shared this idea. The asset manager charges rent to the janitorial company for equipment storage closets in the different office buildings they own. This increase in operating expenses is then passed through to the tenants, which effectively increases rent to the building. Wonder how the janitorial company likes the pass through that they get for the increase in Op-Ex for the space they have to lease??

Decrease Expenses

In addition to driving up revenues on a property, income can go up significantly by controlling the expenses on the other side of the equation. It is really not the focus of this book to explore managing every little expense. Rather, its focus is to explore managing the people that are managing the expenses in a successful fashion. This will be discussed in greater detail as we dive into the roles that asset managers perform. Asset managers are not property managers and keeping a healthy division of those job descriptions is an essential skill of successful asset management. Therefore, separating and allocating duties among high-level and low-level expenses is important for asset managers.

The Balance of Increasing Revenue and Decreasing Expenses

Expense management can be a double-edged sword. On one hand, you may be great at driving down costs. At the same time, you might be foregoing quality of service. Additionally, there are limits to what can actually be achieved. Inputs cost money. Landscape crews all have to buy gasoline and generally pay about the same price for it. Your best negotiation skills will rarely — if ever — alter what someone's going to pay for materials and supplies. Sure, there are purchasing power differences for dealing with larger vendors, and it certainly makes sense to explore these options. I just want to point out that when dealing with the expense side of the equation there is a limitation on how much can be achieved. This is certainly true in commodity-driven services, where most suppliers tend to price compete anyway, and product or service differentiation is hard to achieve.

My first job out of college was a terribly crummy one. I worked for a tract homebuilder that was well known for paying miserably low-wage rates. In theory, this was a great idea for the budget. However, in application it was a nightmare. We all know the old saying, "You get what you pay for." My employer paid very little, and he got exactly that! In general, this holds true in hiring out any service. You can always squeeze another nickel out of any vendor or find someone willing to work for less. Eventually though, you're going to get to the bottom of the barrel. Here is where you start working with what I like to call DDU's: Drunks, Derelicts and the Unemployable! This is where cost-saving starts to work against you. Understanding the relationship between decreasing expenses and quality is very important when trying to achieve company objectives.

Another see-saw relationship that exists for properties is the one between rental revenues and occupancy rates. Moving one seems to affect the other. An asset with 100% occupancy over a sustained period of time can easily justify rental increases. This is wise — up until the point that overall revenues begin to decline from tenant vacancies that cannot be easily replaced. When finding the right balance here, investor strategy is a key influencer to the decision-making process. There are too many variables to cover, but keeping these factors in check with long-term investment goals is critical to the ongoing success of the asset.

Many years ago I purchased a used vehicle that was very hard to find. I found it the day after Christmas, and I got to the lot very early. I called the guy on the way over, and he told me that he had four people coming to look at it that day. I was the first one to see it. I made a quick decision to buy it because the second person already had the keys and was out on a test drive. He said he had two people on their way in from out of town to look at it. I knew he was not playing me. It was a very hard car to find. He made the comment, "I wish I had six of these to sell!" He failed to realize he had it priced too low. Four people converging on the same vehicle screams, "Raise the price!"

Careful consideration needs to be given to 100% occupancy and what it means. It could mean that you have found the perfect balance of price and current demand. However, it could also mean that there are still 10 times the amount of tenants ready to lease space, but there is none left. In this case, you are way under market, and prices do need to go up. A real estate investor who says, "I wish I had ten times the space to rent!" is not maximizing the value of the space that they have.

Increase Intangibles

Intangible assets, such as goodwill, can have a great impact on return to investors and increase property values. However, it is not easy to measure. Goodwill also seems to have a blurred conception in the marketplace regarding what it actually is. I doubt we will clearly define intangibles and put this issue to rest. I don't think it is all that important to do so. I do think it is important to acknowledge its existence and determine how it can bring value to the asset manager and the assets themselves.

Increase Goodwill by Improving the Property

Many respondents mentioned that improving the amenity base also creates goodwill. There can be a lot of truth to that, but I wonder if it is always necessarily the case. When I think of goodwill, I think of something that you don't spend money on. Or perhaps you spend money in one area and reap the benefits in another. Increasing the amenity base certainly improves the value of the property and therefore, increases the price that people are willing to pay for it. But a workout room is simply a workout room. It's the free bottled water post-workout or the chair massage on Friday that creates the goodwill. The money spent on the elliptical trainers is tangible. The feeling that the tenants get after using them is the intangible.

Another mention of how to create intangible value was to install upgrades to common areas. Again, this improves the value of the property, but doesn't necessarily add goodwill to the mix. There are certain things that can be done in conjunction with it that will add goodwill; however, this does not seem to be automatic. For instance, marble-clad walls in a lobby is certainly a nice touch, but the value is measurable and is going to be reflected in the cost. A "free frozen yogurt" machine in the same lobby will certainly have some fans! The cost and value of the tile is tangible. The value of the free desserts is not.

Increase Goodwill by Increasing Customer Satisfaction

Often mentioned in the intangible section was having a customer focus and meeting the needs of the end consumer. This mindset is the start to building goodwill and intangibles. Think about this: All properties have some sort of staff that must operate the facility, but having a friendly staff is optional. A creepy, weird guy can change an air filter or unclog a toilet, but so can a friendly, nice guy. Goodwill is not achieved by doing maintenance, but it is achieved by doing it with professionalism and courtesy. In Chapter 8 these type of staffing and personnel issues will be discussed further.

One asset manager for a Boston-based ownership group had a very creative idea for increasing goodwill with residents of a multi-family community – this idea would work pretty effectively in an office environment as well. Every day, the management office offers free Starbucks coffee with official cups, lids and all, to anyone who comes in to get it. This is not just coffee in a pot in the corner. It is the full on experience of free Starbucks that you might see in the lobby of a nice hotel. This is a nice perk for the residents who live there. What he noticed was that numerous residents also became friendly with the staff because they would begin to see them on a daily basis. Friendliness and repetition built a relationship and increased goodwill. I asked him what they actually spent to provide this perk, and he said about $100 a month. I would estimate this type of goodwill would easily ensure at least one renewal that would not be there otherwise. For each one beyond that, it is additional client retention with no additional cost. Compare that to the cost of compensating an apartment locator for a new resident or a tenant broker for an office user. It's pretty simple math.

Another idea the same asset manager had was to negotiate with different food trucks on different days of the week to be present at some of the office buildings that he managed. He felt that people get sick of the same old food from the same old deli in an office building day in and day out. But offering and promoting different food trucks that would show up on a routine basis offered much more variety beyond that of a simple snack shop. This "perk" to the tenants did not cost him anything but a few phone calls. It did provide value to the tenants in the building. Both the food trucks and the free Starbucks created a breeding ground for interaction between tenants and management for all kinds of goodwill. These types of interactions build the relationships that could be the difference maker when renewal season comes around.

As a matter of fact, I just noticed it in my current office building. They recently chose not to renew the lease with the deli that has been in the building for decades. The very next week, food trucks began to park between the rear exit of the building and the parking garage. I had never before witnessed the amount of people congregating as were there waiting on their food to be prepared. One of the managers of the property was present as well, getting her own lunch and talking to tenants. I can tell you firsthand that this does create goodwill for the owners of the property.

Intangibles can certainly be hard to measure. For this reason, they can also often be hard to focus on and are often overlooked. When you combine intangibles, such as goodwill, with the suggestions on utilizing technology that will be mentioned in later chapters, it is easy to see how small improvements can have a recognizable and meaningful impact.

In summary, you can do a lot to increase the return to investors by focusing on increasing revenues, reducing expenses and creating goodwill. It really is beyond the scope of this book to do more than to offer creative ideas that can assist in these areas. Our belief is that even perfecting these areas will still only lead to minimal increases in the return to the investor. I don't think they should ever be overlooked, but they are not the area of initial focus for us and are not part of the Big Three. All of these efforts (increasing revenues, decreasing expenses and fostering goodwill) should work in conjunction to prevent the erosion of Net Operating Income.

Combating the Erosion of NOI

A good strategy for us to pull information from asset managers was to ask the following question:

"What is the biggest problem you face as an asset manager?"

One unique and succinct response was: "Erosion of Net Operating Income." This gave a pretty good objective for all asset managers to follow. A good asset manager will learn to halt the erosion of NOI.

Picture yourself at the beach. While you look all up and down the coast, waves are rolling in. If it's a sunny day, it could be pretty peaceful. On a stormy day...not so much. The waves that come in are constant. They may change in size and frequency, but they are always there. Your time at the beach may be for a day or a few days. If you are lucky, a few weeks. But when you are gone, the waves continue.

The coastline appears constant in the timeframe you are there — no major changes over the course of a few days or weeks. But this constant ebb and flow of the waves can alter the shape of the coastline greatly over time. Erosion takes place. It's not always observable, but the evidence of it generally is. Perhaps there are pilings to a structure that used to be on dry land and are now in the surf. For the most part, no one would build a structure in the water, but over time the shoreline has changed.

In real estate, erosion is a constant that eats away at income and profits. Erosion is such a good word to describe this, too, because erosion takes place slowly over time. If it were due to armed robbery or petty theft of net operating income, we might have a different defense.

However, because it is due to erosion and takes place slowly, the problem might not be so obvious.

Current market conditions might keep asset managers from focusing on erosion of NOI. For the past few years, in most markets and in most asset classes, real estate values have been driven up and returns have increased as well. This might be causing some sizeable deferred problems for some asset managers. For instance, a very large institutional asset/property manager based out of Dallas offered a thought related to a sizeable increase in one of their line-item expenses. Their belief was that if there was an overall increase in their revenue, the increase in expenses had no impact on them. Therefore, the increase was not perceived as a problem. In a declining market, the effects of this erosion will be harder to ignore and more focus will need to be placed on reversing these trends. Of course, when the market is declining, they will likely have less resources to devote to reversing the trends.

Think about this net-zero attitude mentioned above. Assume the property taxes on one of their assets went up 150%. Now assume that their electrical supplier offers an amazing refund due to 10 years of overcharging them for their electrical service. During the same year, they were able to increase rents by 8%. Expenses only went up 6.5% cumulatively, so they are happy. However, there are too many moving parts to know that this is a good performance by simply evaluating the bottom-line numbers. Sure, the overall performance is arguably good. But it could've been so much better!

I believe a lot of erosion has been largely overlooked during the past few years. Increases in rental revenue has impacted overall performance to such a level that asset managers could deal somewhat irresponsibly with the lesser increases in operating expenses. However, this trend will change in the coming years. The changing market will force good asset managers to separate erosion into two distinct categories addressed in the graph below. Some erosion is market-driven. Other erosion is operational in nature.

Market-driven erosion is due to aging amenities, such as appliances, gym equipment, swimming pools, etc. When this happens, similar renters will be relocating to newer properties. They will also be willing to pay a premium for these better amenities. Operational erosion deals with line-item expenses on an operating budget. Increases in taxes, increases in energy costs and increases in vendor services are operational pieces, which will erode net operating income.

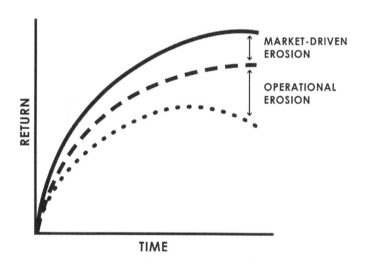

It is important for asset managers to implement the Goldilocks Principle. Simply focusing on NOI is far too broad a goal, and scouring through each little line item is way too inefficient. Like Goldilocks, the focus must be on what is just right. As we go through the coming chapters, try to maintain a middle-of-the-road approach and not get in a ditch. Past experiences can affect present perceptions and performance. The net-zero attitude mentioned previously causes this group to miss out on opportunities to increase investor returns. Further, most erosion straddles both market driven and operational elements masking the problem. For instance, if property taxes increased by 10%, perhaps 6% is due to overall market increases. The remaining 4% is lost to poor management that could be masked by the same drivers behind the market value erosion.

Maximizing Property Values

Overall, the primary way to increase property values is to increase returns or the income that a property is generating. However, sometimes returns are not immediately recognized. A value-add strategy might have a mid-range goal to improve the property. This will take some time. Occupancy can be driven up by better marketing efforts. It can also be improved by improving the amenities. Returns can be increased from operational efforts or investment efforts. Operationally we can increase immediate returns. From an investment standpoint, we can also increase *eventual* returns.

Maximizing the value of any real estate asset involves a lot of moving parts. I think one respondent covered it best. They mentioned a Stephen Covey philosophy that says when you embark on a project, start with the end in mind. With this strategy an effective asset manager tasked with maximizing property value would always be forward thinking about the sale of the asset to the next owner.

Earlier we mentioned that maximizing property value and maximizing returns to investors do not always work in conjunction with one another. That is not to say that they *cannot* work in conjunction with one another, as they often do. It is just not automatic.

For instance, one respondent mentioned the replacement of chillers to one of his properties. We all know that these can be very expensive. He comically mentioned that no tenant has ever walked into a property and said, "Hey, I'm ready to sign a lease here because the air conditioning is fantastic!" Rarely, if ever, will a tenant — or a buyer for that matter — require excellence within the state of the air conditioning systems. Of course, a savvy buyer will want to know the age of all the systems in the building, but it is not likely that it will be an investment that will be fully recouped upon the sale of the asset.

Keeping this in mind, it is important to know the overall objective of the investors that you are working for. An investor with a long-term focus will have a much different attitude towards spending $30,000 to replace the chiller than a value-add investor with a short-term hold. A lot of these types of decisions will surface in the relationship with property management. Things of this nature will be addressed further in the coming chapters, as we identify and speak to the different roles and relationships than an asset manager has.

In certain asset classes it is important to address the tenant mix in properties. Certain types of diversification are necessary to ensure long-term value is stable; this would certainly seem more relevant to office and retail properties than it would multi-family assets.

Probably the biggest reason to always be mindful of keeping the property value maximized (and actually knowing what that value is) is knowing just exactly when to get out. Most asset managers have some degree of responsibility in sourcing and disposing of their assets. We saw a great range in our surveys of the other roles that asset managers actually performed. Acquisitions and dispositions were a very common additional task. Whether it is direct or indirect, asset managers typically have a lot of influence in the timing of gettin' in and gettin' out.

Maximizing property values on paper can be directly tied to maximizing returns to investors. As Net Operating Income rises, while holding the Cap Rate steady, the property value will increase. However, we mentioned earlier that simply maximizing property values is not necessarily congruent with maximizing the return to the investors. Therefore, maximizing property values cannot simply be an accounting methodology. It must also take into consideration the actual physical state of the property and not just what appears on paper.

Relationships

Due to the various disciplines required of successful asset managers, it is extremely important that a good asset manager be relationally connected with many people in his or her given markets. This relationship need was pointed out consistently by higher levels of directors and vice presidents that oversee teams of asset managers. There are many reasons to maintain these relationships and numerous benefits to being well connected with all types of industry professionals.

Brokers

It is critical that a successful asset manager have a key network of commercial real estate brokers within any given market or region that he or she operates. Due to the nature of compensation of real estate brokers, it is feasible for a well-networked asset manager to obtain vast and meaningful information in any market nearly free of charge. The benefit of this knowledge is immeasurable. First, it enables the asset manager to know the markets in which he/she is operating. Friendly brokers are excellent sources of critical information that is not always highly publicized or readily available. This "insider information" can be of huge benefit and provide advantages to you.

Another benefit to a broker network is seeing opportunities and knowing about deals that are coming to market. Being well connected can give you a head start in moving through the process. As we will see in one of the upcoming chapters referencing roles, having numerous lines in the water is essential to finding deals that make sense with your investment criteria. The better connected you are, the more bait you can have out there fishing for deals.

One of the greatest ways of improving relationships with brokers in the marketplace is to simply respond to them. Being available and prompt with written and telephone responses is a critical trait of a good asset manager. Being courteous and professional in a timely manner can be the difference between mediocrity and greatness as it plays out in professional relationships. Because you are continuing to read this book, we know you are absolutely committed to greatness. In the next chapter we will discuss some simple tactics to improve people skills.

Capital Sources

Another important network for asset managers is numerous sources of capital. This is not a book about real estate finance. It is really not our level of expertise nor do we ever intend it to be. Just like dealing with real estate brokers, a good network of investors, bankers, and other debt and equity sources is critical for effective asset management. The same strategies apply regarding professional courtesy, punctuality and timeliness. Keeping a finger on the pulse of these two different networks of brokers and funding sources can greatly contribute to an asset manager's success in sourcing and dispositions.

Property Managers

The relationship of property managers will be discussed in greater detail in later chapters. Successfully managing these relationships is essential in the day-to-day management of real estate assets. Knowing the right people for the right type of asset in a particular market can make life easy and ensure that your goals for a property are properly carried out.

In the next chapter we will discuss motivation in both yourself and others. Understanding this can help you relate better with yourself and with others. The good news is that these people skills are universal. Learning how to improve your relationships with property managers will benefit you in your relationships with brokers, bankers, dog groomers, flight attendants, managers, children, spouses, bosses, rodeo clowns and police officers.

So to wrap up, a good asset manager will maximize return to investors, while maximizing property value through a strong network of real estate professionals. Money comes from people. Our ability to generate money comes from our ability to get people to give it to us. Sure, we may provide them something of value in exchange. But, in general, they are going to do business with people they like. This is why people skills are of utmost importance. In the next chapter we will discuss motivation. Understanding your own and others' motivations is critical in healthy and successful relationships. When you learn to apply these truths in your business endeavors, it will have a very profitable impact.

CHAPTER TWO

MOTIVATION

"Whatever motivates, motivates!"

Dr. John T. Cocoris, Psy.D., has conducted years of study on temperament behaviors. He has written numerous books on the subject. One of the most helpful books to me personally and professionally is entitled *How to Sell Using the Temperament Model of Behavior* (Profile Dynamics, 1988). Before you dismiss the book because you are not in sales, I urge you to reconsider. Everyone is in sales. We all present ideas to others daily and need their buy in. We sell our kids on cleaning up after themselves. We sell our friends on where to eat lunch. We sell our co-workers on helping us complete projects. We sell our friends on listening to a story we want to tell. A key factor in successful selling that Dr. Cocoris's book mentions is understanding what motivates those around us.

In one of my conversations with Dr. Cocoris, he mentioned a mother who was distraught about her son's seeming lack of motivation. Speaking with Dr. Cocoris, she mentioned, "My son doesn't seem to be motivated by anything! All he wants to do is sit on the couch and play video games all day!" He stopped her and said, "I would suggest your son is highly motivated. He is highly motivated to sit on the couch and play video games all day!" Just because someone's particular motivation is not readily recognizable does not mean that it is non-existent.

The last question on our survey read as follows:

Assume you had complete control of your personal and professional time allocation. If you suddenly discovered a way to achieve 100% of your work performance in 75% of the time, what would you do with the 25% of time saved?

The goal of asking this question was to try to understand the motivation of people who work in asset management. We also wanted to give the respondents an opportunity to reflect and better understand themselves. To complete the question, we offered the following off-the-shelf responses:

1. *Make it known that you can handle an increase in your workload.*
2. *Take free time for yourself.*
3. *Spend time volunteering to help a local cause.*
4. *Check calculations to verify 25% is accurate and determine if it is mathematically possible to increase to 30-35%.*

Additionally, we offered a box to check "other" and fill in the blank. I thought it was very interesting that less than 40% of respondents actually answered this question. Our goal in asking this question was to see what temperament blends were drawn to the field of asset management. Since so many people left it blank, I made a few assumptions about non-respondents. Some were likely annoyed by the question and felt it was not relevant to a survey on asset management. Others probably did not want to waste time with it and wanted to move on and complete the survey. I suspect, though, there are many who simply don't take the time to really get to know themselves. So much of our lives we're told what to do. It's almost like we get trained to not let our desires surface for too long. We almost feel guilty or self-indulgent for even considering them. When this nerve gets tapped, it can cause people to move on to the next question quickly.

Since this is a book about asset management and not a self-help study, I do not want to spend tons of time on the subject. However, we do feel that to make it interesting, relevant and, most importantly, to produce change, we need to address it from the standpoint of understanding yourself and your relationships with others. As mentioned earlier, people skills are universal. Learning how to deal with people properly will benefit you not only in professional relationships but in all relationships. Therefore, a cursory evaluation of the subject should be quite beneficial to work, home and play.

If you've never studied temperament behavior, the four options in the question above correlate with one of the four temperaments identified around 400 B.C. These temperaments have been studied and written about for centuries by numerous experts, and I'm not here to offer any new insight into the subject matter. It has been written about enough. I just know from experience that it is an extremely effective way to both understand yourself and to get along with others.

Interestingly, of the almost 40% that did respond to the question above, the answer nearly without fail was the first on the list, indicative of those motivated by overcoming challenges and financial reward. They said they would let it be known that they can handle an increase in their workload.

This tells me two things. First, a pretty large percentage of the respondents fit the temperament that matches the first answer. Although this temperament makes up only about 10% of the total population, an uncanny percentage of them are drawn to high-profile roles that deal with lots of money. It also tells me that the other responses might be perceived as the wrong motivations for someone in asset management. Perhaps people that work in high-profile roles and deal with lots of money feel like they should be highly driven and motivated by it, up for a challenge and willing to take it on.

The chart that follows identifies which temperaments correlate to the answers for the question on page 34. As you will notice, many different versions have been created over the years which label the same temperaments. Although labeled differently, they all describe the same thing. If you have never studied these temperaments, I offer a *brief* summary below. Our goal is not to offer a complete understanding but only a simple suggestion on how to relate and communicate better with yourself and others. The survey answers fit the following temperament descriptions:

THE FOUR TEMPERAMENT TYPES

CHOLERIC	SANGUINE	PHLEGMATIC	MELANCHOLY
Dominant	Influencing	Steadiness	Compliance
High "D"	High "I"	High "S"	High "C"
Directive	Interactive	Supportive	Corrective
Driver	Expressive	Amiable	Analytical

Before we do a quick glance at the different temperaments, I would like to spend a moment on why I think this is important. In the beginning of this chapter it says: "Whatever motivates, motivates!" There really is no right or wrong answer to what motivates someone. Motivations are like tastes. We don't really have a lot of input into what shapes our preferences or motivations. What makes someone like red wine and another person prefer beer? Cake or ice cream? Paper or plastic? Why? My grandpa used to always say, "Different strokes for different folks." It's just the way that it is.

The question of "What is your motivation?" is not nearly as important as the one that asks, "Do you get to act on them?" Does your professional environment allow you the freedom to enjoy the things that make you tick? For instance, the respondents that actually did answer this question said, "Hey, let it be known that we can handle additional work!" But if you're like me and you're motivated by free time, this kind of reward in a work setting might be a noose around your neck!

Again, there is no right or wrong here. People that love to eat chocolate don't practice at it very hard. Just like shoveling in mouthfuls of curry is not going to increase your affinity for the spice if you don't already love to eat it. It's just the way it is. Trying to force yourself to like something is not going to increase your enjoyment of it. Likewise, trying to motivate yourself with something you're not motivated by is not going to work. So if you're motivated by money and extremely high levels of achievement, that's great! It just might not be the same for everyone else.

I started off as a commercial real estate broker many years ago. I did reasonably well at it, but I wasn't great. Most of the people in the office loved making all the money, but I just didn't fit in. Having money was not extremely important to me. Having fun was. Others misunderstood me, but I also misunderstood myself. It's not that I didn't enjoy making money, it's just not something that was going to keep my head in the game day in and day out. At the time, I thought I was weird. I thought something might have been wrong with me. For a long time, I sincerely struggled with the belief that I was unmotivated. I didn't realize until many years later that I did not have the proper incentive structure in place. Everyone else's reward structure of money was not rewarding to me. Years later, I learned that lots of money can buy lots of fun. After that I was back to the races.

Understanding motivations are important for three reasons:

1. You need to know how to motivate yourself.
2. You need to know how to motivate others.
3. You need to know how these are not the same thing.

A little understanding and implementation in these areas can pay extreme dividends in your personal and professional life, so let's do a simple rundown of the four basic temperaments.

Work is Hard, and Hard Work is its Own Reward!

This statement causes some to choke, while others nod in agreement. I don't think there are too many people that actually love hard work for its own sake. I do think those that agree with this sentiment really enjoy the actual effects of working hard. They will gladly take on more work because it will produce more. And they love being productive because it leads to good results, which generally leads to more money. They are the ones that would check the first response above about taking on more work that they can now handle with the additional time they gained.

People wired this way often make the erroneous assumption that everyone else is wired this way too. Due to their work ethic and achievement, they often find themselves in upper-level positions and ownership. They are often other people's bosses. They make good bosses because of their drive and determination. They can make great bosses once they figure out that not everyone is wired like them. Until they get this, they can be quite difficult to be around. If they are unaware of their strengths and uniqueness, they might mistake others for lazy and weak.

Working for the Weekend!

People that fit this bill can be the most visible people in the office. They can appear flighty and unmotivated because they may not seem like they give great attention to their work. This is because work is simply a vehicle for them. Truth is, they are highly-motivated people who are driven by excitement, fun and free time. The second choice above would be checked by this group.

This "free time" motivation can often be incorrectly mislabeled as unproductive, especially by people in the "hard work" group above. This is unfortunate, as "free-timers" can be extremely productive and hyper-efficient. Driven by a desire for personal or free time, innovation and creativity often flow from this type of person. They love to find shortcuts and often find good ones. They like to reward their efficiency with "me time."

"I choose a lazy person to do a hard job. Because a lazy person will find an easy way to do it."

— Bill Gates

I would argue that "lazy" may not be the best word choice, but you get the point. Perhaps the hyper-driven Bill Gates misdiagnoses the hyper-fun people as lazy. Perhaps he views creative people that like to take time off as lazy. Perhaps I am wrong, and he's right. He *is* the multibillionaire.

Those Who Get Things Done

The third option in our survey question is for the many who love the process of doing things. To them the world seems to have an endless supply of action items that need to be completed. And they are great at doing them. Often they claim that they like to help others, but an additional motivation is simply having things to do. They are do-ers, and feel a great sense of accomplishment in getting things done. When they run out of things on their own list, it is not difficult to find others that need help getting things done. If you ask them, they explain it in practical terms. Things need to get done. They do it.

I expect this type of person will be a rare gem in the asset management field. Although they love to do stuff, they generally dislike having to make decisions, especially big decisions. They are quite comfortable being told what to do, and often prefer to have directions given to them. Because asset management requires many decisions that are high on the risk-reward spectrum, this group will often shy away from asset management as a profession. However, they are quite common in property management.

"The most effective way to do it, is to do it."

—Amelia Earhart

Can't Wait to Finish So I Can Check my Work!

Attention to detail is of primary importance to this group. Many in this group are drawn into careers that deal with technical analysis and numbers. These people are often extremely intelligent. They are factual and logical and generally insist on doing things "the right way." Often their work ethic will look similar to the first group. However, the motivation is more for precision than output. Productivity is important to them, but not nearly as important as accuracy. Being profitable is important, not as much for money's sake; it is important because profitability is perceived to be the right thing to do.

The last option for our initial question in the survey suits this group well. They rather enjoy the process of checking facts and figures for accuracy. One of my college friends helped move a girl whose father fit this description. Her father had measured every box and piece of furniture and made a schematic drawing of how everything would fit in the moving truck. This, of course, overqualified him as a mover. Most movers would just shove things in until nothing else fit. Of course, brute force does not work in most surgeries, flight plans or real estate asset management. It's great that many people enjoy technical accuracy and fill in the voids for those who do not.

It does not matter into which category you fit. There is certainly no right or wrong answer. Motivations are personal things and no one's is better or worse than another's. Whatever motivates, motivates. If you get this, you will not attempt to alter your motivation or that of another. You can simply roll with it. Consider the lady who thought her son was unmotivated because he would only lay on the couch and play video games. In reality, he was just not motivated to clean his room. If the controller to his video game was hidden until the room was cleaned, he would then be *highly* motivated to clean his room until the controller was returned. Understanding this simple truth can have a huge impact in dealing with others.

It is critically important to gain personal insight into what motivates you. Why do you do what you do? If you could do it better, how would you allocate your time gained by your personal efficiency? Are you free to do so? If not, then improving your job performance might have horrible implications for you. If you manage others, have you considered what motivates them? When you have a problem that you need help solving, do you know how to motivate others to gain their assistance?

In the case of the free time/weekend crowd, more money could mean more fun for them, but not if it requires more time spent at work. Throwing a party for the hard work crowd is likely going to frustrate them, especially if they are required to attend. Promoting someone in the third group to a position with more flexibility and greater decision-making responsibilities might cause them to dislike being promoted. Giving the "Facts and Figures" group the flexibility to waive certain standards because they have proven themselves will not increase their freedom, but instead could cause frustration.

Once you understand and move past your own motivations, it becomes extremely helpful to understand the motivations of those around you. We'll discuss a lot more of this in the roles and relationships sections in later chapters. Almost all of us will fit pretty neatly into one of these primary motivational groups. That is not to say they can't be further dissected into different levels of complication, but for the sake of simplicity this is a very useful starting place.

It is also important to know that in addition to motivations, each of these groups has their own style of communicating. Within the group, they all have similarities in both communication style and choice of vocabulary. When you understand these and learn to make room for these, it will greatly enhance your relationship skills.

Some of you may now be asking yourself, "What the heck does this have to do with me?" Many of the upper-level respondents to the survey mentioned that maintaining good relationships is key to successful asset management. Asset managers deal with different types of people across many different industries. When you understand that each of these groups will have their own motivations and languages, learning to communicate better with them can make your job so much easier.

Asset managers are in constant contact with brokers, bankers, property managers, bosses, vendors and salespeople, to name a few. In general terms, each of these categories will have similarities within themselves. Further, they will have differences outside of themselves. Brokers will not always have the same motivation as bankers, who will not always have the same motivation as property managers, who will not always have the same as bosses.

Learning to communicate effectively with each of these groups and motivate the people within them can make the multi-faceted function of asset management a much easier pursuit. Also, note that they are not completely industry specific. Nearly all asset managers will fit within group 1, 2 or 4 listed previously. Many property managers will fit into group 3. But temperaments are unique to the person, not the industry. There are exceptions to all rules and trends.

Before we move on and check this chapter off the list, please do not let the fact that you have likely taken a personality profile years ago exempt you from further consideration of this topic. Your ability to plot yourself on some graph does not make you any more of a relational expert than owning a cookbook makes me a chef. I have done this numerous times and have studied this subject extensively, and I still have tons to learn about it and need a lot of practice on the implementation part. I always come back to it, though, because I am absolutely fascinated by how effective of a management tool this is in relationships with others.

I would strongly encourage you to do a personal inventory to get to know yourself better. What really makes you tick? Do you enjoy your work environment and the people that you work around? Is your current compensation structure and incentives program rewarding to you personally? Or is it simply an off-the-shelf solution that your company provides to you and everyone else? Unless you work at a very dysfunctional organization, it's possible that your company's, boss's and your own personal motivations and goals can generally be aligned together very well. However, this does not happen by chance.

Companies are usually built from the top down; therefore, motivations of the leader tend to trickle down throughout the population of the workforce. If your company has four people in it, this type of stuff might be easy to sift through. But in a 50-year-old organization with dozens or even hundreds of employees, there could be a lot of incentive structures that don't match a significant percentage of the employees in the group.

Your company wants you to be successful. I would say in most cases your company wants you to be *extremely* successful. This means your bosses and supervisors want you to be extremely successful. With the proper structure, your success drives their own success. If they are smart, they want you highly motivated to succeed. If your *job well done* is met with a party and vacation, this might be great. But if you want an additional challenge with the upside of additional compensation, this party and time off is not going to speak your language.

Understanding these things about yourself and being able to communicate them to management is critical. Since your company ultimately wants you to be successful, you would think these conversations would go quite well, yet sometimes they don't. Often this is because your comments can be perceived as a threat to the status quo. If the information can be presented in terms of your manager's motivations and language, however, then what may otherwise be seen as a threatening topic may become quite welcome.

For example, let's say you are a High D and you work for a High I personality type. Recently, three of the assets that you manage have had three consecutive quarters of above-average performance. You know based on your experience that you could take on more responsibility. And you *want* to take on more responsibility. So you go to your boss and say the following: "Hey, John. I've done a really good job for three consecutive quarters. I've been killing it! All of the assets that I manage are doing much better than they were a year ago. I know I'm ready for more responsibility. I'm up for the challenge. I'd like you to give me a couple more properties to manage, so I can get my career moving in the right direction!"

In this example, your High I manager is going to interpret much of what you said as a threat. Your drive is going to concern him. No matter how much he believes in you, his real concern is that you will outwork and outperform him and take a lot of the credit for yourself. The directness in your communication could cause the conversation to not go as well as it could.

A better way to approach him is in the following manner: "Hey John, I really want to point out how great of a job you've done in training me to become better at my job. Because of the mentoring and assistance that you have given, I feel like I am ready for some additional responsibilities. Imagine how well it will reflect on you when you are able to communicate that we — as a team — have learned to better divide our roles and accomplish more. It's a lot of fun for me to be able to advance my career in such a team-oriented environment. I really enjoy working for you and the connection that we have. I would love to discuss how you could delegate some additional responsibilities to me."

This is a very simple analogy, but it works. Bosses, co-workers, managers, brokers, bankers, spouses, children, politicians, everyone responds to the language of their own motivation. We will examine this more throughout our discussion on roles, but awareness of this with a small dose of implementation can make your days much easier.

Please, PLEASE, **PLEASE** don't dismiss the impact this can have on you simply because somewhere in your past you took a test and already know what personality type you are. Learn your own motivations and the motivations of others. This is where connections are made on a personal level, and this has the potential to make work so much more enjoyable for yourself and those around you.

CHAPTER THREE

THE CHALLENGE

In this chapter we are going to present a challenge that will resurface towards the end of the book. The challenge is here to make you better. The challenge is here because passing away are the days that allow warm bodies to be successful in real estate. The market is going to become a tougher place in which to excel. This does not mean it's going to be impossible, just more challenging. If you believe a storm is coming, isn't it a good idea to make preparations before it hits? Better to learn strategies now when you can elect to do so rather than later when you might be forced to do so.

If you choose to embark on this challenge, a year from now you will wonder why you didn't do it sooner. The reason you haven't thus far is likely because the opportunity of doing so was in conflict with numerous others vying for your immediate attention. It will produce for you. It will give you great results. It's a challenge not because it's difficult! It is a challenge simply because it requires you to think and act differently. It will challenge you to not work for savings in day-to-day activities. You can certainly do this, but it will not produce anywhere near the results that we will show you.

> *"Do you know what the difference in hitting .250 and .300 is? It's 25 hits. 25 hits in 500 at-bats is 50 points, okay? There are six months in a season, that's about 25 weeks. You get just one extra flare a week, just one, a gork, you get a ground ball, you get a ground ball with eyes, you get a dying quail, just one more dying quail a week, and you're in Yankee Stadium!"*
>
> — Crash Davis in *Bull Durham*

Remember that great scene in that classic movie? What a wonderfully resonating picture of how little difference there really is between mediocrity and true greatness. One hit a week — just one — is the difference in playing at the top or just one step below. This is true in so many professions. Our challenge is based on a few key things that can be implemented that will have a significant impact and produce major results. These results will have a significant impact on the returns that your assets are currently producing. These few key things will be the difference in AA or AAA ball and the Majors. We call it the Big Three.

In our research, some of the questions we asked related to significant expenses from the income statement. There were eight to nine different expenses that were listed and space to fill in any others. They included things like

Payroll/On-Site personnel, Marketing, Insurance, Utilities, Landscaping and Make Ready. We first asked the respondents if each of these items were handled on a corporate, regional or more local level. We then asked each respondent when it came to each of those expenses if they handle them directly/personally, internally or externally. Next, we asked them to rate how much influence that they personally felt like they had in managing each of these expenses. After that, each of these expenses were ranked to determine which of them the respondent felt that they were the most effective at personally managing. Finally, we asked them to rate the bottom-line impact it would have if they were able to optimize their performance in this role.

SIGNIFICANT EXPENSES FROM INCOME STATEMENT	(C) Centralized (R) Regional (L) Local	(D) Direct (I) Internal (E) External	Rate Influence (1 to 5)	Rate Effectiveness (1 to 5)	Rate Impact (1 to 5)
Maintenance (Landscape, CAM, etc.)					
Turnover/Make Ready					
Payroll/On-Site Personnel					
Marketing					
Property Tax					
Energy					
Insurance					
Utilities other than Electric (Water, sewage, etc.)					
Other:					

The desire was to map out the relationships among the different line-item expenses related to Centralization, Involvement, Time Spent, Influence, Effectiveness and Potential Impact. Before we started this project we believed we would see several trends develop when these questions were answered. Most of our suspicions proved true, but other trends that were not predicted did as well.

The following are some of those trends that helped shape the Grand Slam strategy to increase effectiveness in asset management.

Frequency vs. Centralization

One trend that made sense to us is that the frequency of a transaction made the decisions more decentralized than centralized. A very simple example is that grass is usually mowed on a weekly basis per site. We never saw a corporate office dealing with this or any other routine maintenance.

The local staff most always deals with routine events on a per site level. On the contrary, insurance — where buying decisions are made infrequently and most of the time annually — was an item on the corporate ticket across the board. A lot of companies would see some blurring of certain tasks with regional offices, if they existed within the company. Generally speaking, infrequently occuring items tended to be more centralized than their more frequent counterparts.

Frequency vs. Effectiveness

Another trend we noticed, though less pronounced, is that the less frequent someone dealt with an event or transaction, the lower their perception of their effectiveness seemed to be. Regional managers did not really feel competent handling insurance decisions and were rarely tasked with this. Even though this was a big ticket item on most operating statements, it is consistently a corporate level decision and few asset managers felt much competency or influence.

Effectiveness vs. Potential

The relationship between personal effectiveness and importance was somewhat expected, but not to the level we discovered. This was largely the focus behind *Pain in the Asset Manager*. Items with less effectiveness and influence more often occurred in the most potentially impactful areas. This means that a lot of respondents do not feel highly competent in several areas that *could* have the most impact if they were more empowered or confident.

We asked our respondents to rate their personal influence and effectiveness in each area. The answers showed that items that held some of the most potential to be significant were perceived as weaknesses in position or ability. Confidence is key. When people do not feel confident in responsibilities, it can leave a lot of uncertainty, which can lead to a lot of frustration. If the variable here is personal effectiveness, then many should expect a significant increase in performance by gaining competency in a few key areas.

Imagine a guy named Cliff who purchased a piece of land on the side of a mountain. He initially bought it for its fishing and farming potential. Cliff believes that he can make quite a handsome return with his investment property. During the normal course of business, he will later discover an added bonus that was not something he had foreseen.

On the mountainside within his property, there exists a stream, some grassy farmland, a sandy area, some rocky soil and a steep hill made out of volcanic rock. One day while working on his property, Cliff notices a teeny-tiny, shiny little fleck turning in the creek as the water runs over it. He learns that the shiny flakes that he is seeing are small flakes of gold. After this happens, he gets excited and goes panning for gold. It never delivers much. A flake here, a flake there. Soon he is content to go back to his normal course of business.

Another day while tilling the soil to plant a small garden, Cliff turns over a tiny gold pebble. It does not qualify as a nugget, but is exciting nonetheless. It is not enormous, but magnificent compared to the gold flakes. He quickly digs around for more, but he only finds that his exploration benefited the seeds he is planting more than his wallet. In other words, the search for gold was great for tilling the soil, but not for finding more gold.

This random spotting of gold is unpredictable at best. It is not worth his time to pursue wholeheartedly, but one oddity that he does begin to notice is that the closer the proximity to the steep hill, the bigger randomly discovered gold pieces become. Okay, that's nice, but back to work.

One day an expert gold digger comes along and tells Cliff there is gold in that rock formation. "Great! How do I get to it?" he inquires. "You have to have a pick ax." "I only have a small hammer, so I guess I won't be getting to it." "Well, you could go to the store..." "Ah, Ah, Ah, Ah!!! Too busy finding gold flakes and pebbles while fishing and farming to be wasting time busting rocks. Plus, fishing and farming has been great. Why would I take time away from what I am good at and risk working hard at something I am not?"

Months go by and the gold digger approaches Cliff again. This time he has an offer. "How about I help you get the gold, and we can arrange a deal to..." "Let me stop you right there. I am way too busy and have way too much going on. I've got it covered. Thanks, I am good with my fishing and farming. Plus, I hired a gardener and he is finding a little bit of gold for me, and I have an arrangement with him."

A similar conversation takes place every few months. Years pass. A drought occurs, and fishing and farming become less lucrative and more challenging. The gold spottings in the field and stream seem to have dried up. Things get tougher. Making money becomes more challenging. Getting a return on the land becomes more of a pain.

He recalls numerous conversations with the gold digger and decides to reach out to him. He is difficult to reach. He does not return Cliff's call. After several tries, he catches him and reminds him of their earlier conversations.

"Sure," he says. "I would love to help. We need to order equipment and set it up. We will do some site surveys and learn where to find and how to extract the gold on your property. This should take only about six months before we are operational." "Six months?!? I don't really have six months. Fishing and farming are not producing like they used to, and I have bills to pay. I need to get some productivity out of my land." "I wish I could speed things up, but we could have started setting this up a few months ago if you needed money now."

In this simple story above, you see the price we often pay for familiarity. We repeatedly spend time on what we are good at and neglect the things we do not excel in. In the case of the mountain dweller, familiarity blinded him from an opportunity and timing hindered him from taking advantage of a new potential venture once he discovered it. He was content with fishing, farming and a little bit of gold. Often, the biggest hindrance to abundant success is just a little bit of it.

There is Gold in the Side of the Mountain!

Eureka! The story above paints a very good picture of the coming landscape of commercial real estate. A drought is nearing that will squeeze the great profitability that has been consistent for several years. Many respondents commented that they were seeing signs of change coming and are cautiously optimistic (read *"a little afraid"*) of what lies ahead. The good news is that there is gold in the side of the mountain. Now is the time to begin making plans to get to it.

We knew at the start of our research that we would see trends. Our belief was that infrequent transactions with large bottom-line impact would create opportunities in the market for specialization. We suspected, too, that most people were not optimized in the way they handle these infrequent, big-ticket transactions. In other words, opportunities exist for those that can point out the gold in the side of the mountain and help get it. We found numerous examples of great ideas on how to get some of it. But we found no one that had a plan to get it *all*.

This led us to the Big Three of Asset Management. If you will focus your efforts in the following areas, it will create a significant impact on your bottom-line return to your investors.

1. Federal Tax Management
2. Property Tax Management
3. Energy Cost Management

Before you call BS and say that you already do all of these, please keep reading. Just because you have someone who does it for you, does not make them good at it. In the coming chapters we will lay out the strategies that topped the list for handling each of these particular opportunities.

This is where familiarity can cost you. A *been-there, done-that* attitude might keep you fishing and farming with your head in the sand during the coming drought. An open mind could be the difference in being competitive or struggling in the coming real estate climate change. It could be the difference in the correct timing to be able to get the gold out of the hillside. It could be the difference in Little League and the Majors.

The rest of the book will demonstrate how successfully implementing the Big Three as part of the overall Grand Slam could produce a 20% to 30% increase in bottom-line performance for nearly any asset type. Okay, okay, okay!!! Sure, not everyone will achieve this or maybe even come close. But what if you tried and achieved just "25% success" of the best case? What if you achieved just "20% success" of the total? This is still a 6% increase in bottom-line revenue. What other line items are going to produce anywhere near this potential? Let's say you read this book and determine it is entirely crap (and it isn't). You risked 6-8 hours on an idea that you think is completely bogus and will do nothing for you. What other opportunity is even making this type of claim? Where else is the potential to do so presenting itself?

The hardest part about this challenge for many will be that it will require you to surrender your critical and analytical side and embrace creativity. A great trait of asset managers is attention to detail and numbers. But as one respondent said, data will only get you so far. There comes a time when you have to go with your gut instinct.

Information is great, but it is limited because it is never perfect. There is a time for using data to evaluate opportunities and a time for using opportunities to change your results. I challenge you to turn on your right brain, think outside the box, and listen to what some of your peers have done to achieve above-the-norm results.

Remember, the purpose of this book is to make you a better asset manager. This is not a book about extreme discipline and honing your skills. It is a book about opportunistic choices which lead to great results. We tied one of the themes of this book to baseball. Sports are something to which a lot of people can relate. I was always a just-above-average athlete...never a great one. I enjoyed playing sports and excelled at most of them to some degree.

As an adult I once had an opportunity to play Whirly Ball. If you don't know what Whirly Ball, it is more or less a combination of bumper cars, basketball, and jai alai. As I said, I was an average player in most sports. In Whirly Ball,

I was exceptional! I was by no means a great athlete. I have also never claimed to be an exceptional bumper car driver. I was below average in basketball. I never played jai alai, and I am not 100% certain how to even pronounce "jai alai." What made me good at Whirly Ball is that I could see the way the game moved. Anticipation. I knew how to play positions and see where the game was heading. I would not tie myself up with the crowd because this is where everyone was congested and their movement hindered. If you hung around the outer fringes of the pack, the moment the ball popped loose, it would create an opportunity to scoop it up and move the momentum in a different direction without any hindrance.

I am not a great asset manager. I would say I have an above-average understanding of math as it pertains to commercial real estate, but most of you would run circles around my analysis and calculations. I don't know how to talk intelligently about absorption rates and crap like that. I have never worked in the field of asset management. As a matter of fact, for much of what you do I would have little to no advice. I had no previous skills or advice in Whirly Ball either. But when I got in the game, I outscored the next best guy 8 to 1. This had nothing to do with experience! It had to do with creativity and positioning. I could see the landscape of the Whirly Ball court. And I can see certain things about asset management in commercial real estate. This could help you outscore your peers by a significant margin.

Remember what Bill Gates said: Stick a lazy person on a difficult task and they'll find an easy way to do it. Also recall that I don't believe myself to be lazy. I think he misunderstood creative people that like to reward themselves by sitting down and mistakenly labeled them as lazy. I consider myself innovative. Never lazy. I believe if you task a creative and innovative person with a difficult job, you will find an extremely efficient manner to get it done.

Remember, none of this stuff is original thought. The wisest man that ever lived said there is nothing new under the sun. The only thing new about the information here is the way it is packaged and presented. I did not come up with these ideas. You and your peers did. I simply combined and compiled them in a way that will hopefully enable you to view them differently. I listened to your stories. I bounced my ideas off of you and your peers. And just like in Whirly Ball, I knew the right time to break away from the crowd at the moment the ball was most likely to pop out. This uncrowded maneuvering ability led to a lot of momentum without congestion. This led to breakaway opportunities that turned into goals being made. If you will step back and quit working like all the other ants, your perspective will change from a few pieces of dirt: It's transformed into the entire mound.

Some Parting Thoughts

We've talked a lot about trends that we discovered in our research. Some of these might get addressed directly or indirectly in the coming chapters, but I did want to point out a few opinions that we developed in seeing how some of these trends were addressed.

It was uncommon but not rare to find local representatives handling those transactions that occurred infrequently and were quite large. We do not believe this is a good strategy. It is not to say that these people are incompetent and cannot handle this type of transaction; it's just not the best strategy for a few reasons. The biggest reason is that it eliminates buying power. You are not likely to get a huge volume discount from these types of vendors, but every little bit helps. Additionally, as you will see when we discuss the best strategies for achieving real estate investor goals, spreading these out over various local people at various local properties will cause fragmentation and inconsistent results.

The Big Three consists of the three items that can have a very large bottom-line impact for relatively little effort on your part. The Big Three is one leg of the Asset Management Grand Slam. Since all of you have experience with and a familiar knowledge of the key components of the Big Three, we have gone ahead and presented this part of the challenge. However, the rest of the cogs in the Grand Slam wheel involve concepts that will be mapped out in the coming chapters. It would be premature to drop the rest of the Grand Slam Challenge now as some of the concepts and terminology might be unfamiliar. I would hate for anyone to shy away from this challenge because you do not have the benefit of understanding all that it entails. The details will be spelled out in the coming chapters. So read on and see if you are up for it.

CHAPTER FOUR

WHAT'S THE CHALLENGE ALL ABOUT?

"Small rudders turn big ships."

—*Tim Nichols*

You can quote me on that.

As mentioned in the introduction to this book, a guiding philosophy behind my thoughts is the 80/20 rule or the Pareto Principle. This is one of those principles that everyone seems to take for granted. Nobody can really prove it, but no one has really disproven it either. Many people would argue that it holds true in every aspect of life. I believe this is true. I've seen proof of this in many aspects of my own life.

This 80/20 rule gets a lot of attention in my life because I cannot stand to waste time. Many of you busy types might observe me for an afternoon and point out that I waste a lot of time. I do value and spend time on "down time" or "free time," but it is nearly always planned and *always* intentional. Due to the fact that I value being able to decompress, I schedule this into my day. Free time is part of my plan. I generally can afford to do this because I have learned that 80% of my productivity comes from 20% of my effort. I learned long ago to shed the stuff that does not produce any value to me. This improves my results greatly.

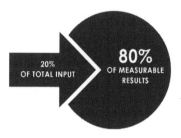

Some of you may be great at this. Odds say that most are not. Pareto says only 1 in 5 is actually good at it. The good news is that if you are not doing this, change is quite simple. If you will put a few things into practice, you can achieve more in less time. What you do with that time can vary greatly. That is why we asked the question that few would answer in the survey. As a reminder, here it is again:

"Assuming you had complete control of your personal and professional time allocation, if you suddenly discovered a way to achieve 100% of your current work performance in 75% of the time, what would you do with the extra 25% time savings?"

What would *you* do with the time? In a nutshell, most everyone's answers will fit into one of these categories: Work more, play more, help more or make sure it (prior work) was done correctly.

The relationship between time and money is very interesting. Consider this: If the only job you could get was meager and just enough to cover your basic needs, most of us would head home the second our needs were met. We are not going to slave away at a sorry job one second longer than necessary. At some point, our time becomes worth more to us than the little bit of money we are exchanging for it. What we can do in our free time is worth more than the poor earnings we receive.

As the pay increases, so is the amount of time we are willing to invest in our professional pursuit. The sacrifice of time becomes worth the exchange. We enjoy the efficiencies acquired with the additional money. For instance, we may work more and not have time to fix dinner when we get home. However, if the increase in money earned gives us enough additional money to pay for food that is already prepared, this is a good exchange. Most of us will pursue this to whatever degree possible.

On the other end of the spectrum is the fact that no amount of additional money can force us to work more. A billion-dollars-a-year salary is not going to be enough if we are required to dedicate 100% of our time to work. There is no time to enjoy the fruits of our labor.

In this chapter we're going to present a new concept and spend most of the rest of the book discussing it in greater detail. In the introduction of this book, I mentioned two common things that have great value to us all: money and time. These are both finite and limited, and they are often in short supply. People complaining about not having enough money are like broken records. They are wearisome to be around. I would argue that people that fit into this category simply do not spend enough time on pursuits that generate more of what they want and need.

I often hear people also complain that they don't have enough *time* to do *whatever*. "I am too busy to take a break, vacation, eat breakfast, etc.!" Horse crap! The truth is everyone has the same amount of time. Days do not last 24 hours for some and less for others. The people that complain about not having enough time, are really quite ineffective at allocating *their* time properly. Therefore, they say things like what was mentioned in the sentence above. "I'm too busy. I don't have time. My time is not my own. Ugggh!" Waaahhh! (That is my baby crying mocking sound!) These are all lies we tell ourselves to make us feel better about our lack of discipline when it comes to planning our schedules.

How do you like it when people say this? "I'm too busy. I just don't have the time!" BS! What about this one? "I'm so hungry, and I don't have time to eat!" Double BS! People that say such things are frustrated, and they commonly frustrate others. Comments like these are outward aggression due to a bit of inner turmoil. Oftentimes people that say such things are not fun to be around. I suggest avoiding them like the plague (or at least like a car full of in-laws). We all get stressed from time to time, but some people tend to live in this state.

I have a pretty good friend that I talk to very regularly. Seems like every time I call him to ask how things are going, within the first sentence or two, he lets me know how busy he is. But he doesn't say he's busy. He says, "busy-busy-busy." When I hear this, I know this is a cover for somebody who's being pretty unproductive. People that are productive talk about their results, especially to their good friends who generally want to hear about good things going on with them. On the other hand, people that are unproductive talk about their challenges. When someone is busy and they tell you that they are busy, it's letting you know that they are being challenged and it's affecting their productivity. Again, there's a little grace here that we can extend to ourselves and to others. We all get busy from time to time. But those who perpetually live in this state need to personally challenge themselves in the area of effectiveness.

Return on Time

Not one respondent in our questionnaire said that Return on Time was a metric that their company used to evaluate effective asset management. ROI, ROE and Cash-on-Cash Return were pretty common. No one mentioned Return on Time. Sure all of the ROI & ROE type equations are annualized returns, so time is considered, but not the amount of human effort that must be put forth to achieve them. Mathematically, Return on Time might be a little bit difficult to gauge, but conceptually it is a phenomenal idea! I'm sure one of the reasons it is not tracked is because it is not necessarily asset specific. What it does gauge is a return of a sum over a period of time based on effort expended.

I grew up in the 1980s. Back then, you could produce a comedy movie for a relatively small sum of money compared to today. Tons of slapstick comedies with relatively big names were produced that did not cost a small fortune. *Armed and Dangerous* was one of these. It starred John Candy, Eugene Levy and Meg Ryan...so no small potatoes here. One funny scene in that movie demonstrates the concept of Return on Time quite well.

John Candy plays a police officer who is wrongfully suspended for stumbling across police corruption involving some of his superiors. He catches them stealing a TV, and they in turn frame him for the crime. While on suspension, he is forced to take a role as a private security officer. During an orientation meeting with Guard Dog Security, the new trainees are congratulated for entering a $12 billion-a-year industry. One of the idiots in the peanut gallery asks the question, "You mean I'm going to make twelve billion dollars?" "No! You're gonna make $4.60 an hour, which is starting pay for everyone!" Sighs filled the room. "You work 10 hours, you make 46 bucks!" Frank Dooley (Candy) asks the question, "Now, let me get this straight. If I wanted to work, say three billion hours, I could roughly pull in over twelve billion dollars? If I was eager enough and put the time in."

This models greatly the concept of Return on Time. I'm absolutely certain that both your boss and mine would be totally ecstatic if we were to communicate to them that we had a plan for raising $12 billion. However, once they realized it would take 3 billion hours to accomplish, their ecstasy would turn to chagrin. Working nonstop without any breaks for meals or rest, this would take over 342,000 years to accomplish. $12 billion sounds great, until you realize that it might take until the earth kills off the next round of dinosaurs before it actually comes to fruition. Therefore, returns must be measured over the amount of time and effort that it takes to produce them.

Assuming asset management required you to perform 50 tasks, the Pareto Principle says that you could achieve 80% of the value of all tasks, by focusing on the top 10 things (20%) on the list. To be 100% effective (and no one is), you would need to perform everything on the list. But to be 80% effective, you need only address the top 10 things on the list. As mentioned earlier, this is a universal principle that seems to apply in every aspect of life.

Assuming each of these 50 conceptual tasks took the same amount of time to complete, it would be futile to deal with the bottom 10 items on the list and wasteful to address the second-to-the-last group of 10 from the bottom of the list. Return on time is really a measure of overall effectiveness. When prioritizing your tasks for any given goal, it is very important to keep this concept in mind. This is what Pareto or *Mr. 80/20* stumbled across in his theory.

On a side note, Pareto did not coin the phrase "Pareto Principle." Romanian-born management consultant Joseph M. Juran did. In 1941, Juran came across the work of Vilfredo Pareto. Pareto first *applied* the efficiency model when he noticed that 80% of the land in Italy was owned by 20% of the population. He first *observed* this distribution when noticing that 80% of the peas in his garden came from 20% of the pods. Pareto applied his efficiency distribution across many other areas of his interest. He was an Italian engineer, sociologist, economist, political scientist, and philosopher. Here are some examples of how his principle plays out:

- 80% of results come from 20% of efforts
- 80% of activity will require 20% of resources
- 80% of usage is by 20% of users
- 80% of the difficulty in achieving something lies in 20% of the challenge
- 80% of revenue comes from 20% of customers
- 80% of problems come from 20% of causes
- 80% of profit comes from 20% of the product range

- 80% of complaints come from 20% of customers
- 80% of sales will come from 20% of sales people
- 80% of corporate pollution comes from 20% of corporations
- 80% of work absence is due to 20% of staff
- 80% of road traffic accidents are cause by 20% of drivers
- 80% of a restaurant's orders come from 20% of its menu
- 80% of your time spent on this book will be spent on 20% of this content
- 80% of your success as an asset manager will come from 20% of your actions
(http://www.businessballs.com/pareto-principle-80-20-rule.htm)

Recall the initial purpose of reading this book: To be better, increase returns to investors and increase property value, *blah, blah, blah.* Consider the goal of increasing return to investors. Ideally, this would consider the ratio of Return on Investment. However, as in the case of Frank Dooley at Guard Dog Security, we don't have 5,000 lifetimes to produce this result. So we must consider a measurable timeframe to allow ourselves to do this. This may be built-in to our ratios of how we evaluate asset performance, but it does not consider often, if ever, the amount of time it takes us to do so. I'm not talking about years to measure some type of return. I'm talking about the time wasted trying to squeeze a nickel out of something that prohibits you from spending time on a task that will generate a measurable result.

Now apply this to maximizing property value. If you are investing money to improve a property, 80% of the value added should correspond with 20% of the improvements. If this is the case, special attention should be given to the top 20% of the list. Identify these items, and you will know where to channel most of the resources and where to scrimp!

Apply these thoughts to relationships: 20% of your professional relationships supply 80% of the value. Focusing on and nurturing these key relationships is the best allocation of your time. Shedding the relationships on the lower portion of your list should be a profitable undertaking. My grandmother passed away over 10 years ago. I still remember something she used to say over and over again at appropriate times, Life is too short to spend it with people you don't like. Well, that's a great statement. I'm going to quote her on that:

> ### *"Life is too short to spend it with people you don't like."*
> ### — Hazel Page

Consider this principle and how it applies to all aspects of your life. Much of what we focus on is really quite pointless when you consider the time it takes. This will not only apply in professional areas, but personal areas as well. Managing your life according to this principle should free up tons of time to reallocate towards activities that are important to you.

This principle was instrumental in developing the Big Three and the Grand Slam Challenge of *Pain in the Asset Manager*. Of course, there are numerous items on the income statement for any real estate asset. But if you're looking to make improvements (increasing actual money generated), 80% of the results are going to come from 20% of the drivers. Therefore, a small handful of changes should create dramatic results. In talking with numerous managers, owners and even some vendors, we stumbled across some extremely opportunistic ideas and strategies that have created spectacular results in the areas of asset management.

At the beginning of this chapter we pose the question: *Why a challenge?* Why does the challenge need to be presented in order to alter behavior? I don't know; it just does. Anytime we do something routinely, we have a tendency to take for granted the things that become familiar. Familiarity often breeds complacency. Complacency can get us in a rut.

I spent one year of my college career living in a fraternity house. This house was a bit unusual in that it was on several acres of land outside of town. I was not the only one with a four-wheel-drive vehicle, and many of us would use the several acres to drive around what came to be known as The Track. The Track was a lot of fun when it would rain and get muddy. Many parties ended with people four-wheeling around this *mud-fest.* One particularly dry evening, we became bored with the regular track and began doing power slides across the field in between. This was a lot of fun until my truck slid across a deep rut and flipped over. Fortunately, no one was severely injured. Getting out of that rut caused a major upheaval, ultimately flipping a vehicle. It was a pretty dramatic event.

It is easy for us to get stuck in ruts. Getting out of ruts, not so easy! Often the results can be pretty scary. It takes us from something familiar and comfortable to something that is unknown. Most of us like to give our attention to things we are good at. We tend to avoid things that cause us problems. It is so much easier for us to focus on our strengths rather than our weaknesses. But this is not a good habit. Sometimes our best results will be created in unfamiliar territory. If we're not willing to get out of our comfort zone, we will certainly miss opportunities. We must think outside of our own box.

Asset managers are often creative and analytical with a decent set of people skills. All of these traits are beneficial and have been identified in this study as qualifications for good asset managers. Although having both creative and analytical traits are beneficial, they are often in conflict with one another. Additionally, they both seem to have certain moods associated with them. At any given time, people who function in either of these characteristics seem to do so exclusive of the other. When someone is being creative, they are generally not being analytical and vice versa. And sometimes we are wearing our analytical hat when we should be wearing our creative one. Most of us are pretty good at self-regulating most of the time. Notice I say most of the time. None of us are *always* firing on the right cylinder.

Derek Jeter, Lebron James, and Tom Brady are all super-exceptional athletes of our era. (As a matter of fact, last night I watched Tom Brady march his team down the field in a final, last-minute drive to set up another game-winning field goal.) These athletes are quite well-known and play at the highest levels of performance in each of their different sports. They are the amazing ones. The elite. The greatest of the great. There are dozens of others we could add to the list. They are worshiped for their talents, and they make millions upon millions of dollars. They play different sports. They have different skills. But they all have one thing in common: They all have a coach. They seek guidance from people other than themselves.

None of their coaches have anywhere near the athletic ability that any of them do. If their coaches did, *they* would be *competing* and not coaching. But you never heard Derek

Jeter bashing his batting coach for being a lesser hitter than he was. We've never heard Tom Brady say to Bill Belichick, "Oh yeah, why don't you get out here and do it!" This would be stupid. Coaches are not great at being athletes. They are great at developing athletes.

Coaches exist not only in every sport but in every profession worldwide. There are people out there who can simply make you perform better. They don't have to be better than you at performing; they just have to be better than you at spotting opportunities in your performance to adjust. They also need to be competent in guiding you in how to make changes. Without this skill, they are not very effective. With this skill, they can assist anyone in honing their abilities and usher them into greatness.

Who is your coach? Yes, you. You manage tens of millions of dollars. I'm sorry, hundreds of millions of dollars in real estate assets. This is an enormous undertaking. Who is guiding you through this process? Who is challenging you to be better? Who is looking under your hood pointing out the chinks in your armor? The greatest athletes in the world have coaches. Should you? Oh, you've got this? You got it all under control, all taken care of? You don't need any help? The greatest athletes in the world all have the coach thing in common. They also have this in common: They know they don't know everything. Another thing that they all have in common is that they have had coaches at every step of their career — not just when they became major league bad-asses. Are you waiting for your induction into the American Asset Manager Hall of Fame before you get a coach?

One of the best reasons to have a coach is because we inherently spend time on unproductive pursuits. We will oftentimes get sidetracked on menial tasks from items far down on the bottom 80% of our list. Coaches, counselors or guides help us give our attention to things that will ultimately be for our own benefit. They can take an inventory of what we are doing and help channel our efforts to one of the things further up our list. My goal in mentioning this is not to get you to go out first thing Monday morning and hire a coach. It is, however, to get you come to the realization that not every great idea is nestled in between your two ears. Even the greatest concepts in your head might need someone to help develop the necessary skills to bring it out.

There are some great concepts that will be presented in this book, that may or may not be familiar to you. You may have heard some before, tried some before, talked about them before, etc. But until you have implemented them with success and achieved a return because of them, your past experience has no future value and should not dictate your future actions. So as you read the ideas and suggestions throughout this book, please do so with the mindset that none of us have perfect information. That's a nice way of saying that you don't know everything! If you will allow someone who is not the asset manager that you are to guide you through a process, it will create some pretty dramatic results.

With changes coming to today's real estate climate, it's a good time to begin looking for some creative concepts and ideas that will guide you through the coming storm. The changing market will not only create new challenges, but also opportunities. So as we wrap up this chapter, I would like to present one last question: Are you coachable? Or do you "Got This"?

CHAPTER FIVE

THE HATS MATRIX

"Secrecy is the enemy of efficiency,
but don't let anyone know it."

—*Rick Ocasek*

I doubt anything presented in these coming chapters is revolutionary in thought. However, I have never seen it presented in the manner that we are about to present it. I doubt we have unlocked any great secrets of the universe, but as we present roles, relationships and responsibilities of a typical asset manager, perhaps the unique format will shed some new light on familiar ideas.

As mentioned in previous chapters, we inquired of many people in asset management as to which metrics their company used to gauge effective asset management. Returns were often gauged by initial investment, equity, cash infused, etc.; however, we never heard the concept of the return on the amount of effort expended. Without a measure of human effort and effectiveness, it is difficult to evaluate an asset manager's performance as compared to opportunity.

Recall that time and money are two valuable resources for each and every asset manager, and we know that both are often in short supply. We also know the greatest way to overcome scarcity is with efficiency. During our research, we got the idea to create a grid or a scatterplot. In the chart below, we place frequency of occurrence on the X-axis. We then placed impact on bottom-line performance on the Y-axis. This graph shows the relationship of frequency (time) and return (money). The simple scatterplot became the basis or framework for gauging the concept of Return on Time.

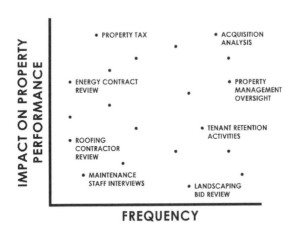

If you draw a line from each axis into the field, you create four different sections or Quadrants. Each of these Quadrants can become a classification of duties, roles or relationships inherent in asset management. In the upper-left Quadrant, we have items that come about infrequently and have a significant impact on returns. These have a low level of occurrence but a high level of value. In the upper-right Quadrant are items that occur frequently and have a significant financial impact. These happen a lot, and they mean a lot. In the bottom right we have frequent occurrence with less value. Finally, the bottom left captures tasks that are infrequent and of little value.

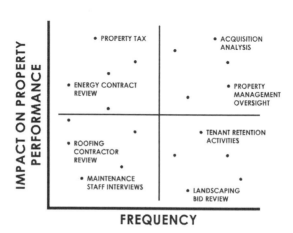

FREQUENCY

Inherent in this Matrix is the concept of the Pareto Principle. Of course, not everything simply fits right in here neatly. However, from a time allocation standpoint it is a good idea to break things down in these simple groups. Assume for a moment that this graph represents asset management tasks. If you plotted each task on the Matrix, in theory, each would fall within one of four Quadrants. Taking this approach, we should notice some similarities among the different tasks that fall within each Quadrant. Once every task made its way onto the graph, you would then assess the overall potential value that could be provided based on the frequency with which each item occurs.

Items that occurred closest to the intersection of the two axes would likely be far less important to an asset manager than things that appeared on the upper right. A reasonable person would infer that the higher something rates on the Y-axis, the more attention it should be given. The graph below breaks down each Quadrant with Roman Numerals I, II, III and IV. And if you wanted to create a to-do list based on the Pareto Principle, generally you could start with Quadrant II and then move to Quadrants I and III. Finally, items in Quadrant IV would be listed. Following this order would generate a to-do list created from the top down.

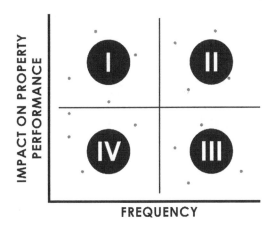

Of course, there would be some exceptions to the rule listed above. However, this would be a pretty efficient way to generate a to-do list in the order of overall potential value. I mean why spend lots of time on something that doesn't happen very frequently or provide a lot of impact to earnings? If Pareto said that 80% of the results of something come from 20% of the causes, then I am looking long and hard at most of my results to come from Quadrants I and II with the emphasis being on Quadrant I. Why not the other way around? Why wouldn't very frequent and very impactful tasks create more impact overall? Specifically, why wouldn't items from Quadrant II be at the top of the list of potential impact?

I would say things in Quadrant II do create the most impact, but asset managers have highly specialized ways of performing those tasks well and most organizations do these quite efficiently as part of their core competency. It is likely that you, and most other asset managers and companies, have already capitalized on most of these efficiencies. Perhaps the greatest *marginal* impact is what lies in Quadrant I. I think Quadrant I has the second-most TOTAL impact to success, but it offers the largest OPPORTUNITY for additional positive impact.

Additionally, I would argue that oftentimes familiarity brings complacency. It's not because most of us are lazy or stupid, but it goes back to the ruts that we mentioned in earlier chapters. We are all creatures of habit. With few exceptions, most of us tend to resist change. Most of us seriously resist significant change. We also tend to learn from our mistakes. This causes us to get really good at what we do most often. As our skills develop, so does our impact on job performance. Once we string along a series of wins, we develop a track record of success. We simply become better at what we do.

The good thing about this is that we become much more efficient at the things we do frequently. One of the problems it tends to create is that we can begin to operate with blinders on. Our specialized skill-set forces us to focus on our core competencies. The tendency on the other side of the equation is that we tend to ignore what we are not great at. If the only tool in our toolbox is a hammer, then everything begins to look like a nail. Or perhaps we only look for nails to hammer. Or worse, we begin to smash everything in sight with a hammer thinking everything will respond in the same way.

When I was in high school, I remodeled houses. I actually started doing this at the age of 13. It started off small, but after a few years my older brother and I were able to generate a decent amount of money for a couple of young kids. Before the days of Lowe's and Home Depot, there was Builders Square. Before that, there were building supply stores named Furrow and Handy Dan (at least in Houston anyway).

One day I was at Furrow in southwest Houston picking up some materials for a job. I saw a buddy of mine at the help desk asking a pretty stupid question. He asked, "Is there any way to make a drill work like a saw?" "Not very well," came the reply. I kind of did an internal chuckle. I knew better than this. Probably because I had asked the same dumb-ass question a few years earlier. At some point though, I learned this was not possible. He was just now in the process of finding it out. He had the wrong tool for the job at hand. He also had the wrong attitude. He didn't even ask where to look at saws. After his idea was shot down, he just left the store. So he had at least half an hour invested in getting this question answered. More importantly, he had a task that needed to be performed. Getting back in his car and driving home wasted another 15 to 20 minutes. He has the same board at home that still needs to be cut and the same stupid drill that's not going to work like a saw. He could've purchased a saw to cut the board for $25 or $30.

God only knows how much time he wasted before he figured out how to make the cut.

As stated above, oftentimes familiarity breeds complacency. Again, it's not stupidity or laziness that's the cause. It likely has more to do with being able to recognize the incremental value of your time and resources being applied in a different manner. In the case of the high-school kid at the hardware store, he was stuck on an idea or a need to make a drill act like a saw. He was not calculating the value of his time taking trips back and forth while he contemplated *how* to make a drill work like a saw. I guarantee you that he never figured this out.

Items that fall in our Quadrant II have the potential to create the same challenges for us. We are so busy performing these tasks, we seldom step back to look at opportunities that might exist outside of our normal MO. This book is not about teaching you how to find monumental efficiencies in your day-to-day routine. Honestly, I really don't think that is possible. I think those efficiencies have already been uncovered. And they're already being implemented. *Pain in the Asset Manager* is about finding unique opportunities outside of your normal bag of tricks.

Relationships

Let's view this Matrix through a different lens and look at it as it applies to relationships. Imagine that every professional relationship you have can be broken down by frequency of engagement and impact on value. In likely the same manner as above, you could create the Pareto relationship list by moving from Quadrants I through IV. In theory, 80% of the value in having these relationships would come from 20% of them. Of course, some exceptions will apply. But, by and large, most of the opportunities, deals or exchanges you are doing occur with a small number of people compared to the whole.

Try going through your LinkedIn profile. I was forced to do this yesterday. I had coffee with a guy who wrapped up our meeting going through my LinkedIn page and asking me one-by-one for referrals with different people that I am connected to. I cannot explain why, but this was quite uncomfortable for me. What really struck me as odd, though, was how many of the connections I have very little to absolutely no contact with whatsoever. Out of 15 to 20 names he went through, there were only two to three that I have any ongoing involvement with. This could be good or bad depending on how you look at it.

Recall the quote I used from my grandmother, "Life is too short to spend it with people that you don't like!" If you want to have better and more meaningful relationships with others, you don't have to try really hard. Further, it's a pretty futile effort to try at all with well over half of the people on your list. This is not to say that they are not important. It is to say that their relationship with you is not important. Sorting this list can be a delicate task. Your mother does not need to appear on the bottom of the list. Your mother-in-law might.

Professional relationships can be handled in much the same manner. Just because a relationship provides little monetary value to you, it doesn't mean you scrap it completely. A better strategy is to wisely monitor the amount of time you allow to be spent interacting with a particular person. Do you have a money list? In a professional sense, this might not be a bad idea. It might seem a little shallow, but it could be a highly effective tool in your personal time management. I think in the back of our minds we all know who is on this list. It's not a bad idea to get it written down and out into the physical universe. For some reason, getting things in print has always helped guide me in my endeavors. Actually, this book started to become a reality when the initial ideas behind it began to be written down.

Roles

We are now going to apply this Matrix to the different roles that asset managers play. For the record, we could apply this to many different roles people have both within and outside of asset management. It could be applied to any profession. The principle behind it is really time allocation. There are many universal truths that could apply. Breaking down roles and responsibilities for any job would be beneficial — especially as it relates to the amount of value it provides compared to the amount of effort it requires.

As we began to conduct our research, we saw trends develop and determined a pattern, if you will, for how we would present the information. We wanted to create something that made sense and was easy to remember, labeling each Quadrant to give meaning to the roles performed within each one. We thought of names, colors, shapes, analogies, pictures, titles, etc. Hopefully, what we came up with meets our goal of being simple and memorable.

I have four children. And man, are they a lot of work! As they get older, they get a little bit easier to relate to. Our roles as parents have changed, and every day our relationship with our children changes as well. When it came to naming each of our children, we wanted the names to be both unique and significant. To accomplish this, with each new birth my wife discarded the top 100 list and started from there. What we came up with are uncommon names that are significant to us.

My oldest son was named after his maternal grandfather. His name is Michael Hays Nichols, and we call him Hays. Next is my second son, Asher Laurence. He and I share the same middle name with the exception of the spelling and a *possible* distinction in pronunciation: I pronounce mine the same as his, so it rhymes with "Florence." However, my middle name is spelled L-a-r-e-n-c-e. My wife gives me crap about this all the time. The way she says it, it rhymes with "Clarence." She argues that that is how it is spelled, and this is why we had to add the "u" to our son's name. Next, we have our only daughter. Her name is Taviah Selette. Selette was my wife's grandmother's name. Taviah was a cool name that appeared in *D Magazine* about the time we needed a name for our daughter. Lastly, we have Salem Hoyt. He is definitely a little Salem!

For years, our kids have visited their grandparents during the summer in Galveston, Texas. They now spend a week or two at the beach hanging out with Nana, as Papa passed away a few years ago. After one of these visits when my parents brought our kids back, I noticed my parents referring to the four of them as HATS; in order: Hays, Asher, Taviah and Salem. Initially, I thought this was kind of cute, but honestly, it annoyed me a little. Can't put my finger on why, it just seemed like a silly acronym. My dad was the type that was always thinking of nicknames for people. Perhaps that was part of the annoyance. I thought this label was kind of silly. But it stuck! My mom still uses it to this day to grab their attention. When she yells "HATS!" they all come running. So even though it is silly, it is very effective. It is also quite easy to remember.

This became the basis for the name of our efficiency Matrix. No, this is not named after my children. It does coincide, however, with the different types of engagement required for each Quadrant of this efficiency Matrix. Below you see a chart that encompasses the guiding theory behind *Pain in the Asset Manager*. I give you the HATS Matrix:

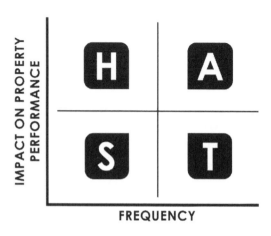

Remember my highest priority of the Big Three is to help you identify and implement opportunistic strategies that will generate a large return. As we dissect the HATS Matrix, you will actually see that all of these opportunistic returns come from one specific Quadrant. Earlier we showed how this HATS Matrix can be applied to tasks and relationships. Now think of it in terms of different roles that an asset manager may be responsible for. Sticking with our analogy in baseball and implementing the Grand Slam, let's assume this original four-Quadrant Matrix represents a baseball organization. Within that organization, many different people have many different roles. Each of these roles are very important to the organization as a whole. Just like each of your roles as an asset manager are very valuable to the asset as a whole or a group of assets as a whole.

Now let's break up the HATS Matrix based on its intention: the relationship between time and money. We will cover in greater detail each of these Quadrants I – IV in the coming chapters. For now, I want to offer a cursory glance. As we go through these, keep in mind they can apply to any profession. They can also apply to many aspects of asset management. Just like the Pareto Principle can have many applications, so does the HATS Matrix. As we make our first pass through this, think of the different HATS as methods for addressing the things that fall into each category.

Hire

In the upper left Quadrant I, we have items that occur infrequently but have significant value. You can think of these as actual expenses, the way you manage these expenses, or even the relationship you have with vendors that manage these expenses. Because of the infrequency of their occurrence, this is something you really are not involved in every day. It is not generally a good use of your time to develop expertise on things that are dealt with so infrequently. It is also risky to handle things directly in areas that have such high potential value when experience is lacking. Besides, there are others that tackle these things on a daily basis. They have developed the same expertise and efficiency in these things as you have in your high frequency tasks.

For instance, if you have problems with the toilet in your house, you might get out your toolbox and pull off the back lid. However, if your air conditioning unit starts to falter, you are probably not going to start tinkering with it with your electric screwdriver. A new toilet might cost a couple hundred bucks. Because the value is low, you might be willing to risk messing with it — and possibly messing it up more — prior to calling out a professional. A new air-conditioning unit could cost several thousand dollars. If you screw up one of these, you're out some big bucks. Toilets are not extremely complicated pieces of equipment either. There are not that many moving parts. It is reasonable to develop the skill set necessary to fix your toilet problem. In many cases this can be done in very little time. Air-conditioning units can be extremely technical. Most people that service them have some level of professional qualifications that took some time to acquire. For these reasons, you would **Hire** a professional to address high-value, low-frequency concerns. You would bring in a specialist that has a skill set that is not worth your time to develop.

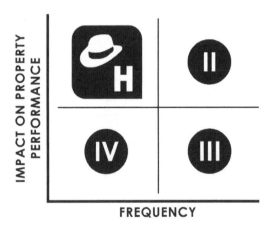

On a baseball team, the owner of the team is responsible for making personnel decisions. The owner hires and fires people on his staff. When dealing with things in this Quadrant, picture yourself wearing the owner's hat pictured in the graph above. When dealing with hiring decisions, it is essential to make good choices. The owner carefully selects the leaders and performers who shape the organization. Because the transactions are infrequent, the relationships with these people will tend to last one to several years. When selecting, it is important to pick a good horse because it will generally be a lengthy ride.

Attack

In Quadrant II in the upper right corner are items that have significant value and occur frequently. This is where we become highly effective and highly efficient. These are the things that should win the majority of your focus. Because of the repetitiveness, these things allow us the time to develop the necessary skills to address them head on. This is where the majority of our day-to-day activities will be spent. This is the area where we should spend time developing the majority of our professional skills. Continuing education classes could take place in this arena.

There is a lot of value in developing the expertise to address the things that occur in this Quadrant. This is due to the fact that once you develop a skill, you get the opportunity to repeat it over and over again. This is the concept that Henry Ford applied to the assembly line of automobiles. Instead of having a general carmaker perform multiple tasks, each had targeted and specialized training that enabled each worker to perfect and perform a laser-focused skill. Had he only needed one vehicle, perhaps he would have "MacGyver"-ed one together with bubblegum, popsicle sticks, and a set of bicycle tires. But it was definitely worth the time to develop a system of specialization that would enable him to repeat successes. This mindset pioneered the way for the mass production of automobiles.

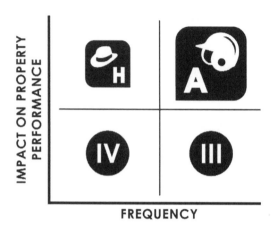

In this Quadrant, you go on the offensive and **Attack** the things that occur here. In our baseball analogy, we will put on a batting helmet and step up to the plate! Many different things can actually fit into this category, and they may look quite different from organization to organization. Across several companies, core competencies may vary greatly. What may be routine for one group could be quite specialized for another.

Train

In Quadrant III are items that occur very frequently but are not extremely impactful. Individually, these things may not have significant value. Cumulatively, they could have a very sizable effect. For this reason, these items should get quite a bit of attention. However, they should get a limited amount of *your* attention. These things should be outsourced to people that you have a significant amount of influence over. The people that address these issues will need guidance and direction to carry out the objectives of the ownership groups.

When dealing with the relationships associated with this Quadrant, it is necessary to **Train** or coach people properly. It is also necessary to have the right people in place. This can make training a much easier task. In the baseball organization, the coaches are the ones that train the players to be better at their roles. As an asset manager, there are numerous people that must be trained to carry out the objectives of your company. When you are working towards this end, picture yourself wearing a coach's hat to properly train those around you.

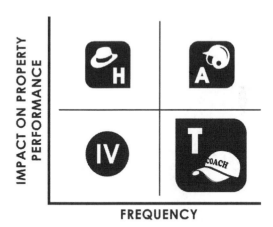

Certain things towards the top of the Quadrant may have a much higher value than things at the very bottom. So, the attention these items get may vary to some degree. Even if the value is inconsequential, the frequency of occurrence will generally keep them from being completely ignored.

Scrap

Finally, we get to Quadrant IV. Here things appear infrequently and have very little value. These things might always occur in the bottom 20% of Pareto's lists. These things should be ignored most of the time, but obviously they can't always be ignored. These are the necessary evils. Very little time should be invested in these areas and relationships.

The air conditioning unit in my home has a filter. This filter should be changed about four times a year. It actually gets changed more like two to three times a year. I try to purchase pretty decent filters for it, but I could not tell you where the last ones came from. I tend to buy a handful at a time. I don't spend a lot of time doing research. I also have no idea what brand I currently use. I have no idea what I spent on the last ones. I don't have a relationship with anyone that supplies these for me. I don't plan on developing a relationship with anyone that supplies these. Are you getting the picture?

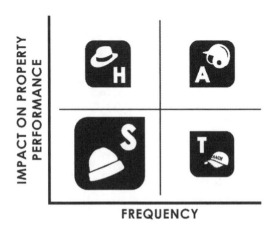

Because of the lack of value and frequency, it is not very beneficial to invest much time in this Quadrant. Even performing at an optimal level within this Quadrant will produce negligible, if any, measurable value. When addressing the things that occur in this category, picture yourself wearing a garbage man's hat. What does that look like? A toboggan cap, of course. And much like taking out the trash, run these items out to the street and forget about them. It is **Scrap.** And the root of scrap is crap!

I hope you like the concept of the HATS Matrix. I believe it is a simplistic way to help provide significant value in prioritizing our time. The next four chapters will take a more in-depth look at each Quadrant of the Matrix. We will discuss in greater detail the feedback that we received during the course of our research. I am confident that it will provide great benefits to you as you strive to increase returns for your investors and property values. My goal for you is that by the end of this book that you are ready to step up to the plate, swing for the fences and hit the Grand Slam.

CHAPTER SIX

HIRE

If the statement "small rudders steer big ships" holds true, this Quadrant is the sea in which those ships sail. This is really the make-or-break Quadrant. We mentioned earlier that the real estate market is soon to undergo some changes. Everyone has been riding high, but market conditions will change, and demand and asset performance are certain to normalize. When this happens, efficiencies will be needed to ensure that returns keep pace with expectations. Many will be scrambling, guessing what action to take to keep providing returns. Don't be left guessing.

Although items in this Quadrant are high-potential, they are often overlooked. As a matter of fact, nearly all respondents gave attention to only one or two of the items that will be discussed in this chapter.

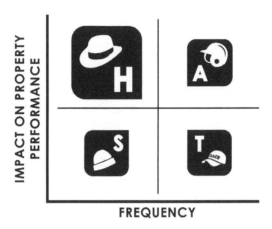

Additionally, asset managers graded their personal impact low on the actual items that they did address. So it is typical to address only one or two of these items and even then, not seemingly very well. Not one asset manager surveyed claimed to have addressed all of the items listed in the Big Three. Perhaps a handful of them do, but it is certainly not the norm. The obvious question to ask is why, in general, do asset managers *not* give these more attention? If I had to provide a simple answer, it would be that even though they are quite large, for the past few years they have not been the highest marginal return.

Marginal return *refers to the additional output resulting from a one-unit increase in the use of variable inputs, while other inputs are held constant.* (Thanks Wikipedia, oh, and Google for getting me there!)

Remember Economics? Simply put, there have been better areas to focus on because of the opportunities that have existed with above normal demand in the recent real estate cycle. For instance, Renovations and Make-Readies have gotten more attention, as the need for more and better units, spaces, etc. has taken attention away from costs that have been rising at a much lower rate. In other words, more money has been made making improvements than has been lost due to rising costs. As this pent-up demand stabilizes, areas of focus for this highest marginal return will shift. In the next phase, cycle or generation, the best opportunities to maximize returns will come from Quadrant I aka Quadrant H. When this happens, be ready to put on your Owner's hat, and Hire some good people.

We have all heard the phrase, "If you want something done right, you better do it yourself." The guy who invented this likely doesn't spend much time with his kids and certainly has not learned to maximize his Return on Time. Outsourcing does not make you incompetent. Just the opposite. You could develop the skill-set and resources needed to address these issues, but you also understand the concept of Return on Time. This understanding enables you to hire the right specialist for the job. To a specialist, any one of these tasks is high-frequency because it is their focus all day every day. They have developed the tools, fostered the relationships, and studied the regulations that allow them to complete these tasks efficiently. Specialists do not come free, but their superior performance and efficiency will likely add value beyond what you could obtain individually. Since these are high-impact tasks, a specialist *should* provide additional value far greater than what they cost. Your goal in hiring the right solution should focus on maximizing this surplus in value, compared both to what you could achieve individually, as well as what other solutions are available in the marketplace.

So what opportunities exist in the Hire Quadrant of the HATS Matrix? We have identified and previously mentioned the Big Three, and these items have contributed to the Grand Slam of Asset Management. They have already been mentioned in the Challenge Section, but now we will delve in a little bit deeper.

Recall the three key areas which can create a significant impact on your Bottom-Line Performance:

1. Federal Tax Management
2. Property Tax Management
3. Energy Cost Management

Combined, these have the potential to increase bottom-line performance by a very significant amount. We will actually demonstrate how the combined potential could be as high as a 30% increase in bottom-line performance. If this sounds like a ridiculous amount to you, then this could be welcome news. As we go through each one of these components of the Big Three, we will spell out strategies that are critical to the overall success of making it all work.

Federal Tax Management

There might be a handful of tasks that fall under this heading. However, there are two that stand out that are in sync with the Pareto Principle. Both of these deserve quite a bit of attention, but the first one will likely have a much greater impact on your bottom-line performance. Federal Tax Savings potential is often overlooked as a core strategy. This causes many owners to leave opportunities on the table, along with a lot of money, in the form of tax deductions. A cost segregation analysis involves an engineer completing a comprehensive study of the individual depreciation schedules of the various components of a real estate asset. This enables the owner to take advantage of accelerated depreciation in a more aggressive manner than the standard straight-line depreciation values.

Cost Segregation Studies

A Cost Segregation Study is a federal income tax tool that increases your near-term cash flow in the form of a deferral by utilizing shorter recovery periods to accelerate the return on capital from your investment in property. Whether newly constructed, purchased or renovated, the components of your building may be properly classified through a cost segregation study into shorter recovery periods for computing depreciation. In a nutshell, the benefit is provided by carving out – into five, seven, and 15-year useful lives – certain qualifying portions of your building that are normally buried in 39 or 27.5 year schedules.

You may be wondering what type of properties actually qualify for this benefit. Any property that is newly constructed and placed into service within the past five years will qualify. Additionally, so will a property that is *purchased* or *acquired* within the past five years. The value needs to be over $500,000. Renovated properties with large amounts of added features, high-end finishes or necessary capital improvements can also qualify.

The theory behind the tax advantage is simple. Shortening the useful life of components allows you to take a greater expense in the earlier years. Depending on asset type, the percentage of components that can be reclassified into a shorter schedule commonly ranges from 18% to 40%. The following table addresses typical reclassification percentages in the majority of the asset classes managed by respondents.

PROPERTY TYPE	RECLASSIFICATION %
Apartment Building	20% to 40%
Office Building	20% to 30%
Retail Property	18% to 30%
Industrial Property	22% to 45%
Mixed-Use Property	18% to 45%

(CREDIT: www.engineeredtaxservices.com/cost-segregation/)

An additional benefit of a Cost Segregation Study that is often overlooked is the fact that you can go back and recapture past years' benefits by adjusting previously-filed tax returns. This can be extremely attractive with assets that have been in your hands for three to five years.

Many people think that to take advantage of this cost-segregation study it has to be applied on a new asset. This is not true. An asset that has been owned for just a few years will provide a much greater tax advantage in Year 1 as previous year's tax returns can be amended and the savings recaptured. This would allow a multi-year, carry forward, sizable recovery in the first year applied.

Most participants of the survey admitted they do very little to nothing to take advantage of this Federal Tax benefit. It is not unreasonable to generate an 8% to 12% increase in effective per-asset earnings in the first year where a Cost Segregation Study is applied.

The cumulative effect of recovering multiple years could be quite significant and yield a 30% to 50% increase in bottom-line revenues (when compared to NOI) when initially implemented. Of course, accelerating the depreciation schedules will remove the benefit in later years. However, most owners' planning and buying horizon is much shorter than the straight line model of 27.5 or 39 years.

A Utah multi-family property experienced the following results with a Cost Segregation Study. An $8.259 million property was able to increase bottom-line performance by over 10%. In years one through five, the Cost Segregation Study enabled them to reduce taxable income by $104,845 per year. This resulted in a $41,937 tax savings (at 40%). Because they were three years into ownership when the study was done, they were able to reap the benefit of over $125,000 in bottom-line savings during the year the study was completed.

The graph that follows demonstrates the tax savings of a typical Cost Segregation analysis when applied. Take note of the fact that they are 15 years into ownership of the asset before the effects of accelerated depreciation has a counter effect to the bottom-line earnings.

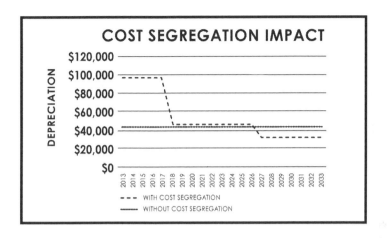

This is quite favorable to nearly any owner, especially those whose hold periods are within this timeframe. In addition, there are other tax benefits that can be uncovered at the same time as a Cost Segregation Study. Two of them are somewhat noteworthy, and we will mention them briefly.

Energy Tax Benefits

This benefit will not work for everyone, but it is worth evaluating. It is called the Energy Policy Act of 2005, and the benefit is referred to as the 179D deduction. It is offered to incentivize owners and developers to create energy-efficient buildings. It applies to commercial buildings, apartments (four or more stories) or commercial energy renovations either placed into service or rehabbed after December 31, 2005 but before January 1, 2014. The deduction is for improvements that will reduce total annual energy and power costs with respect to the interior lighting systems, heating, cooling, ventilation, and hot water systems by 50%. However, partial deductions are allowed. If a property qualifies, it can range from $0.60 to

$1.80 per square foot tax deduction. A 200,000-square foot property could receive a tax deduction of $120,000 to $360,000, giving a bottom line increase of $48,000 to $144,000 in the year applied.

Abandonment Incentives

Another tax benefit that is often overlooked is abandonment of existing systems. In certain remodeling projects, systems that are demolished still may have a lot of unallocated depreciation on the books. If handled properly, the value of this unapplied depreciation can be written off upon demolition. Not taking advantage of this will leave you depreciating assets that you no longer have. This is a one-time transaction, but the results can be significant. It is not uncommon for non-existing assets to carry several hundred thousands of dollars on the books. Taking advantage of this can lead to a very sizable tax savings. Any line item that can impact the bottom-line revenues in large amounts should be given careful consideration. Both the Energy Tax Benefits and the Abandonment Benefits would be uncovered with a proper Cost-Segregation Study by a competent engineering firm.

Property Tax Management

Federal Tax Management may have the biggest savings in the initial year applied, but Property Tax Management, handled properly, will provide the best savings and benefit over the life of the asset. There are numerous strategies and opinions in the marketplace on how to effectively achieve the best deal on property taxes. But before you have the right strategy, you must have the right mindset. We've heard many people say, "I only want to pay what's fair." However, when it comes to property tax assessments, none of it is fair! No one is fairly taxed. Very few properties are taxed at actual market value. If you do not believe this, please contact me. I will have buyers ready to close, within one week from Friday, on every asset in your portfolio at the assessed value on the tax record for each asset.

The first thing to consider in an effective tax strategy is this: Everyone is taxed below market value. Now that this is settled, let's move on. As I said, to have the right strategy you must have the right mindset. And the right mindset says there is no fair amount to tax. It is all arbitrary. There is no perfect way to accurately assess unique properties in comparison with one another.

The basis for fair assessments really lies in circular logic. A property's value is derived from another property's values, which has been derived from other property values based on the same information. Knowing this, the best we can do is to plot them on a graph with comparable properties. However, this can only be done in theory because no one really knows the actual "fair amount" in comparison to the assessed amount. Everyone has their opinion and a butt! Ha-ha.

In the following graph, we take this hypothetical analogy and create a scatterplot. On this scatterplot we can plot every asset within a market that can be used as a comparable asset to the actual target asset. Since we assume that every asset is below-market value, we can plot each asset on the graph at a fraction of its actual market value. Again this is hypothetical, but some will be closer than others. In order to see how you stack up to other assets in the same market, you would have to draw a trend line of all the different values.

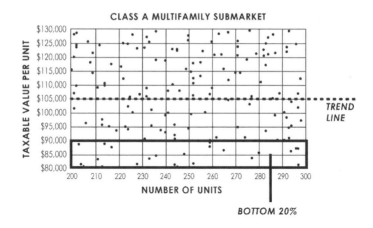

Half of the assets would fall above the trend line, and half would fall below. In actuality, the ones above the trend line are subsidizing taxes for others. In a like manner, the ones below the trend line are being subsidized by others. Where do you want to be? Simple math tells you below this trend line. Ideally, you want to end up in the bottom 20 percent. Getting here is not accidental — it is intentional.

Due to the subjective nature of property tax assessments, anyone and everyone can argue their point of view until they're blue in the face. When this puffing-of-the-chests is over, the kangaroo-court-like panel offers a decision, which nearly invariably aligns with the people who assemble them. This is the Central Appraisal District.

The goal of the Central Appraisal District is to push these assessed values up toward the market values. The goal of any owner or their tax representative should be to push this assessed value below both this enigmatic market value and the conceptual trend line on the scatterplot. Success in this area involves a tactical strategy for bringing it about.

The unique and unfortunate thing about any Property Tax Management service is that it is impossible to evaluate service providers in an apples-to-apples comparison. It is not possible to engage two different people with the same directive during the same year. You must choose an agent. You can only obtain one result each year. So it is impossible to compare two different providers at any given time; this is a known fact and somewhat of a dilemma.

One Atlanta-based multi-family management respondent to our survey offered a great suggestion. He concluded that while it is impossible to compare two different consultants' performances on the same property, it is quite simple to compare your consultant's performance to the rest of the market. This offers an accurate way to let you know how well your tax representative is performing in comparison to the rest of the market, not just how your property is performing when compared to itself year-to-year. With this measuring stick, only about one third of the representatives in any given market will generate a favorable result. The rest will range from just above average to way below the market when compared to all properties.

The unfortunate thing about this industry is that anyone with a pulse can show a positive result. Even a pretty crappy job generates a better result than no job at all. And someone who performs poorly, out of self-preservation, will report the result in a manner that weighs favorably for him or her. Unfortunately, this may not weigh favorably for you! So remember, the second thing to consider in an effective tax strategy is to compare your results to the market and not the assessed value.

The next tool in your belt for an effective property tax strategy is to piss, pound, punch and scream until you are convinced there is nothing left to squeeze. This is how you get your final result way below the trend line. This "take no prisoners" mindset coupled with the right strategy will deliver the best results that will keep you in the bottom 10% to 15% of the market. And this is where you want to be. Once you realize that everyone is assessed below market value, you want to be as far below the "market trend line" as possible.

The right strategy says we're going to push this decision until all possible value has been recaptured. If you're not willing to fight to claw back every nickel, then you probably won't.

The Appraisal Review Board is not the final decision-making authority in property tax hearings. The courts are. If your strategy does not involve this piece of the pie, or if you wait until after the meal was served to determine if you want dessert, then you are not fully prepared when you sit down to the dinner table. Of course you do not have to bring an attorney to the hearings, but you best let them know that he's coming to dinner!

One respondent had a very good example of how this was achieved with four properties in the same submarket in the DFW Metroplex. They are a multi-family developer that owns Class A Properties in the $25 to $50 million range. One cluster of their properties lies in a submarket of a major county in North Texas. Taking all of the comparable properties reported by property managers for rent comparison in the nearby area, we created the chart that appears on the next page.

The aggressive "CAD to Courthouse" strategy was implemented on all four of the subject properties listed as Properties 1-4 in the chart.

	2013	2014	% Δ	
Property 1	$25,669,681	$25,850,000	0.70%	
Property 2	$28,650,000	$29,125,000	1.66%	Median: 2.03%
Property 3	$35,841,425	$36,700,000	2.40%	Mean: 2.63%
Property 4	$37,450,099	$39,612,500	5.77%	
Comparable 1	$16,700,000	$18,600,000	11.38%	
Comparable 2	$24,000,000	$25,000,000	4.17%	
Comparable 3	$40,220,000	$41,856,000	4.07%	
Comparable 4	$19,000,000	$21,200,000	11.58%	Median: 8.33%
Comparable 5	$47,000,000	$49,200,000	4.68%	Mean: 8.40%
Comparable 6	$24,000,000	$26,000,000	8.33%	
Comparable 7	$35,500,000	$38,000,000	7.04%	
Comparable 8	$38,800,000	$45,000,002	15.98%	
Comparable 9	$49,749,130	$53,899,130	8.34%	

The initial hearing did not create the desired result of the consultant's target value as the assessed value. This led to litigation described above with the ultimate possibility of going to trial to generate the desired result of the value of the MAI Appraisal that was ordered. In all but one case, the CAD eventually stepped back from their original assessed values. This generated acceptable values in three of the properties at 0.70%, 1.66% and 2.4% increases in assessed values. The average increase of the three properties was 1.59% when the rest of the market was 8.4%.

The fourth property actually did go to a jury trial. The verdict led to an increase on Property 4 of 5.77%. This was better than the average, but a bit higher than the other subject properties. Overall, this still gave the respondent an average increase of 2.63%, nearly 5% below the average of the rest of the market.

The previous case study shows what can be done with a comprehensive strategy from start to finish. When you know the best decision should come from the courtroom, you can often push this result upstream. In order to do this, you have to show that you are prepared to pursue it to the end of the road. Having all of your ducks in a row is critical from the get-go. Without this, you will risk being perceived as the little boy who cried wolf.

Based on the best practices reported to us, we believe the best results are achieved with the following line-up:

1. Property Tax Consultant
2. Trial Attorney
3. Appraisal

These professionals working in conjunction with one another will likely be able to deliver the best result on a consistent basis. Remember, the goal should be to consistently remain in the bottom 10% to 15% of the market that your asset is in. To do this consistently, it has much more to do with the fight in the dogs than the facts on the page. Once you concede that the numbers are all fluff and arbitrary, it's easy to comprehend how the process is far more important than the statistics. To keep your properties on the lower end of the scatterplot, you must consistently press them in that direction. You do this by consistently being the path of most resistance.

Energy Cost Management

This one should get a lot of attention in certain states. In regulated states, the benefit is non-existent. In deregulated states, however, they can be quite substantial. Again, this item was often overlooked by many of the respondents. When discussing Energy Cost Management with a Regional Vice President of an out-of-state multi-family investor, his response was, "We don't even look at energy!" This surprised me. They have over 35 Class A multi-family assets in the state of Texas. Texas is a deregulated state. With this type of buying power in one state, it's arguable that they are leaving quite a bit of money on the table. Numerous suppliers would love to get their business. They are not even addressing this.

Energy brokering is not a new thing. Most people are quite familiar with it. It seems many don't take advantage of it. The industry as a whole is quite unregulated. I'm pretty certain that anyone who says, "Hey, I'm an energy broker" has met all the legal qualifications of becoming an energy broker. Because of this, compensation is unmonitored and all over the board. Industries such as this tend to attract participants that like to take advantage of consumers' ignorance. This type of practice can be quite lucrative in the short run. However, it can breed resentment. There are no required disclosures from the brokers to their clients. As you can imagine, this leaves a lot of opportunity for consumers to indirectly pay their brokers more than what most people would consider a normal return for the services provided.

I still see it as a wise decision to evaluate the opportunities related to Energy Cost Management. You should just understand a little bit about the market before you jump in. Energy rates are pretty volatile. When the prices move in the right direction, they can create a great opportunity for users to lock in at lower rates. Typically, these commitments are two-to-five-year terms. Because the rates are commodity driven, the benefits are often the result of market opportunities rather than asset management skills. However, they can still provide very significant increases to net operating income. Combining multiple sites to increase buying power can create savings as well. This would be skill driven and not solely the results of market changes.

There are numerous professionals in the marketplace that claim they can help you in your Energy Cost Management. Brokers are common. They will shop your usage to numerous suppliers. Suppliers will work with them to bid for your business. Because it is unregulated, the broker's compensation can be added to a deal in a number of ways. There are no required disclosures to the consumer. In the right market, the broker might save you tens of thousands of dollars while paying himself hundreds of thousands of dollars. For this reason, it is important that you trust the people that you work with.

A typical Energy Broker transaction will be a one-year to five-year arrangement. This will be followed up with a phone call a couple of months prior to the agreement expiring from broker to consumer to renew at the most competitive rates available at the time. This is a very poor strategy because rates fluctuate. Review the following history of average electrical rates in the state of Texas:

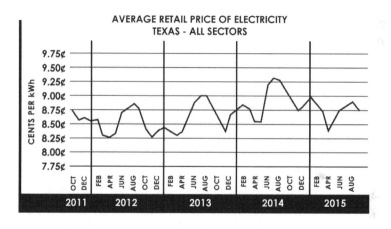

(*Source: U.S. Energy Information Administration*)

Someone who entered into the agreement in the middle of 2012 would have done so at a high point in the market. Additionally, their renewals one or two years later would occur at peak times as well. Their contracts would be addressed when their rates are the highest. This strategy would result in someone paying more for energy than others in the market.

A managed energy plan would enable you to extend your service agreement during the troughs. This would allow you to take advantage of declining rates even if you are not at the end of your agreement. When dips occur, you can either blend the rates of what you currently have with current market rates and add a term or add a completely new agreement with a future start date on top of the current one. This type of managed program will lower your overall costs by frequent monitoring. The right broker or consultant will bring the opportunity to you.

Look at the case of one Texas respondent who employed this Managed Energy Cost strategy. They originally entered into a two-year agreement during March 2011. During the course of this two-year agreement, they extended the agreement at a lower rate approximately one year into the term. Due to their energy procurement having a managed solution, they saved 30% on their electricity costs instead of having to wait to renew at the market rates at the time of their agreement expiring.

To summarize, it is important to understand that energy is a commodity. Opportunities are generally created by fluctuations in the market. As stated previously, opportunities can also be achieved by wholesaling your use to a single provider. Pricing will not typically vary greatly from one supplier to the next. However, with significant use, even a small price fluctuation can have quite a large impact. This is why this line item merits your attention. People who overlook this opportunity are missing out on some pretty simple to get returns.

Summary

Each of the components of the Big Three is unique. For different reasons, they are all something that an asset manager should generally outsource to a specialist. The Federal Tax Management strategies are extremely technical. They also require a professional engineer to perform the due diligence and create the report. For this reason, few — if any — real estate investors will have an in-house solution. The Property Tax Management strategies require various professionals to assist. Ideally, the different professionals would have a history and working knowledge of each others' practices, as well as the different jurisdictions of each of the properties. Energy Cost Management is best handled by someone with extensive relationships with numerous suppliers. The commonality that all of these have is that it is not worth your investment of time to replicate their skills.

Because some of the services offered are not often a part of the normal real estate transaction, huge potential exists for those who have yet to take advantage of these services. We believe this Big Three approach to asset management *will* deliver a 5% to 10% increase in bottom-line performance. It *should* produce a 10% to 20% increase. It *could* create 20% to 30%, and with the perfect storm, who knows, maybe 40%. Regardless of the final outcome, any of those improvements from least to greatest would generate a better return than anything we will list in the coming chapters. 80% of the effect comes from 20% of the cause. These items here should be getting the lion's share of your attention.

.

CHAPTER SEVEN

ATTACK

The second Quadrant of the HATS Matrix is the one reserved for your area of expertise. This is by far the hardest one for an outsider to identify exactly what fits where. Because every individual and every company has special skill sets, core competencies and expertise, every situation is unique. More important than figuring out what fits in this Quadrant is the concept of spending your time on the things that matter most. And you know what matters most. Following the goal of this book, the activities that you focus on day-to-day should both increase returns to investors and maximize property values. These goals do not only apply to the tasks in this Quadrant, but these goals should be mindful in all of your daily activities.

A thorough breakdown and analysis of this Quadrant is, unfortunately, the one where we will provide the least amount of insight to you. The good news is that it is also the one you should need the least help in. Your core competencies are just that! At a heart level, they are what you are extremely good at. Your ability to function well here should help you maintain investor returns and property values. For us to find great opportunities in areas that you are theoretically an expert in would be a somewhat arrogant goal for us to take on.

In the HATS Matrix, following our baseball analogy, this Quadrant is represented by a batting helmet. It is where you are on offense. It is what you do day-to-day. It is the area where you Attack the important activities that bring the best returns. On the baseball team, if you are a big hitter, you will spend a lot of time in batting practice. It is similar in asset management. A lot of times it seems as if you are practicing. Not every day is game day.

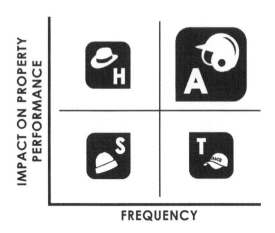

In our research we discovered that many asset managers are responsible for additional tasks beyond the "managing of real estate assets." The one most frequently mentioned was sourcing deals and new acquisitions. Depending on company structure, involvement in finding new opportunities could range from providing supporting information to Acquisitions Directors all the way to being solely responsible for the identification and pursuit of new opportunities. Regardless of your depth of involvement in finding new deals, maintaining relationships with the outside world is quite important.

At the very least, a good asset manager will see opportunities to dispose of existing assets. While kicking tires to determine the best exit strategy, it is important to be forward thinking. If you can sell an asset for a huge gain, but can't find a place to put the money, this might create a problem. One respondent from a large development group in Houston really exaggerated the importance of asset managers having great relationships. Another offered an analogy that brought a lot of clarity on how to manage these relationships.

I like to fish, but I am no great fisherman. I have a good friend named Matt who is great at fishing. If it weren't for him, I would probably never go. I'm glad he often asks me to join him. He likes to fish so much that he is constantly throwing his line in the water. I, on the other hand, like to fish less. I enjoy the scenery, floating on the water, the breeze, the beer and the conversation. Because of this, when we're out fishing together I generally do not cast my line in the water as much as Matt does. Who do you think catches more fish?

Matt's success is not solely because he is a better fisherman than me (although he is). There is certainly a skill to it, but this skill also causes an enjoyment that keeps him casting his line more frequently than I do. We both enjoy it, but he will likely always out-catch me in fish on any of our trips. I am okay with this. I generally will outpace him in the beer and conversation portions. In addition to skill, Matt's ability to catch more fish has much to do with his line being in the water more than mine.

It is very similar when it comes to success in the relational aspects of asset management. Every contact you have with the outside world in different professions could be viewed as a line in the water. I'm not sure what the average deal-viewed-to-close ratio is, but I'm sure it is quite low. Most of you look at numerous deals to find just one that makes sense. Because of this low hit ratio, it is important to maintain good relationships with those that are bringing them to you. We mentioned this briefly in the chapter on motivation and people skills.

It is one thing to be nice to people. It is another to maintain a mutual level of respect and professionalism. As I mentioned about Matt, a line in the water was one thing, but the art of fishing was another. It is certainly an art to keep outside brokers bringing new opportunities to you – especially when the likelihood of getting one over the goal line is pretty insignificant. Just like in fishing, asset managers need the right balance of not wasting time and keeping them interested in the bait. This too is an art.

Relationships with lenders and capital sources are critical as well. One high-level respondent with a team of asset managers stressed the importance of getting the right financing structure for a deal. There are numerous funding sources, and creativity in generating the right capital stack can be the difference in creating a win-win. Relationships are critical. Understanding motivations can separate you from the pack. Placing the right deals in front of the right people can be the difference in being at bat late in the game versus watching from the dugout.

In general, people do business with people they like. If people like you, they will want to work with you. A while back, someone gave me a great suggestion on how to get along with others: BE NICE! It really amazes me how rude some people can be. We can all do it from time to time, but some people have made this the rule and not the exception. I guess there are some people out there that have had enough success in their careers they can afford to be a-holes to others. They might argue that it works for them. What really stumps me though are young people with no track record and tons of attitude. Any and all of us would be much better off, more enjoyable and more profitable by investing some time in developing our people skills.

We deal with people every day, although as technology increases we are dealing more with devices and less with people. I personally have such an annoyance with the interruptions that technology brings to relationships. Here's an idea if you want to set yourself apart and stand out in today's environment: When you are around other people, don't get out your smart phone. You will stand out because you are offering undivided attention. No one does this anymore. We have become habitually fragmented forms of our historical selves. It really is a shame. I saw a genuine Christmas card one year where a family posed, all with their heads down, looking at their smart phone, tablet or some other device. The dad was even holding up his finger offering a "give me a minute" gesture.

We could argue that these devices bring so much convenience into our lives. And to some degree they do. But there is also a time and a place for them. Here's another idea: If you MUST whip out a device in a meeting or in the presence of someone else, simply acknowledge that, "I hate to be rude, but this is important." Even this courtesy will make you stand out. Most people do not even see that it is rude anymore. The important concept here is to be courteous and make people want to be around you. That — coupled with professionalism and doing what you say you are going to do — is an unusual trifecta in today's marketplace. We mentioned this earlier in Chapter 2 on motivation. The concepts presented there are mostly overlooked, but they are so simple to implement.

The book I mentioned earlier, *How to Sell Using the Temperament Model of Behavior*, could just as easily be called *How to Communicate Effectively with Others*. It is not the only resource like it. I am sure there are numerous others. And they will all likely mention similar things. If you learn a few of these simple skills, you can relate the importance of rave parties to an underwater marine biologist.

Asset managers typically have a small number of different groups of people they routinely deal with. Most of these groups will have a different culture, value system and language. Being able to understand and relate to each of these can be very beneficial in your career. I am not saying it's a good idea to try to pass yourself off as one of them. This can be pretty risky. I liken it to the English-speaking guy in a crowd of Spanish-speaking people that suddenly takes on a Spanish accent on his English words. It provides absolutely no benefit to the Spanish speakers to speak to them in English with a mock Spanish accent that these morons commonly place on it. This is at best comical and often quite embarrassing.

I am not an asset manager. I have already stated this. I can do math, but most — if not all of you — would vastly outperform me in this area. So me writing a book on asset management could mean that I am taking on a huge risk.

However, I am not coming into your world, dissecting it and trying to tell you how to do it better. Instead, I am throwing out a small handful of high-value opportunities that I found which many are not taking full advantage of. But it is important for me to communicate them in your terms. I like fun. But selling you all on the free-time and fun that can be gained by picking up on those opportunities would often fall on deaf ears. It is important for me to mention the efficiency that can be created, as well as the improvements in procedures and the reallocation of corporate resources for improved returns.

In the same way, the brokers, bankers, property managers and vendors that you deal with all tend to use a separate and unique vocabulary. This uniqueness is not only based on a professional vernacular, but more often on the motivations of the people that are drawn to this particular job. Think about this. If you're looking for capital for a project, you are not going to impress a banker by talking to them about a 30% return. They want certainty. Just like a hedge fund is not looking for your 6% guarantee. For the rest of the chapter, I will offer some general ideas on how to deal with different people in your sphere of influence. These are certainly not absolute. But overall they will help communicate with those people that are drawn to the different job descriptions that you likely deal with on a daily basis.

Brokers

If you are involved in sourcing or disposing of deals, real estate brokers are critical to your success. These guys are pretty simple. I mentioned earlier that I used to be one. Even though I didn't fit the common mold, I still spoke the language and understood the motivations common in that group. There are exceptions to every rule, but understanding these trends can help you navigate through these relationships better and communicate more effectively.

Real estate brokers tend to be very brief, decisive and often controlling. They can be very firm and unyielding and are often very good negotiators. They tend to have clean and polished appearances. If you are in their office, you will likely see their resume on their wall (along with a power slogan and a picture of Donald Trump). The great thing about these people is that they are pretty easy to work with. Although they may come across as such, they are generally not mean-spirited people. They simply have a drive inside of them to get results and to not waste time. They appreciate people who are brief and direct with them. Don't spend a lot of time on small talk unless they offer it first. They can tend to be pretty friendly in a rushed and hurried manner. Don't be surprised if they cut you off midsentence and move on to the next thing. This is generally just their mind telling them to accomplish something else.

Most people that fit into the broker category hate being taken advantage of, not being in control and being perceived as weak. They can become easily annoyed, especially if they feel their time is being wasted. They will interrupt you. Don't get offended. By all means, don't lose your cool. These are the alpha dogs. One thing to know about working with them is that you do not need to be friends first. They are much more likely to be professionally tied with those that navigate through transactions quickly rather than those that hang out with them at the swimming pool.

Bankers

If it is up to you to find people to participate in your deals, then you need to learn to get along with bankers and other lenders. This can be a little more difficult, but is certainly not impossible. People that are guardians of other people's money tend to be more closed and reserved. They are usually very organized, and they are often serious in their expression. When talking, they can be mild yet inquisitive and come across as being suspicious.

When working with them, it is important for them to know that they are making the correct and best decisions. If a particular deal or transaction is not a fit for them, do not spend time trying to convince them that it is. They will base their decision solely on the facts. They will need lots of information. Your best selling skills will rarely trump this need. Closing them on the spot can be very tough as well, as they tend to need time to think about their decisions. When calling on them, do not cloak your intent behind verbose and crafty pitches; this frustrates them, as they would like to know your intent from the very beginning.

These guys are not big risk takers. Additionally, they do not like conflict. They fear making wrong decisions and being viewed as incompetent. When dealing with them, they can come across as negative. Be prepared for lots of specific questions and skepticism. They expect and value quality and attention to detail. If there are holes in your deal, they will find them. And they will want these holes filled before moving forward. If you gloss over their specific questions, you will lose them. This devalues their need for information and desire to be precise. Relationships with these guys are hard to develop, but they are also hard to break once developed.

Property Managers

In general, people drawn to property management roles tend to be personable and cordial. Most of the time they are nonassertive, and their tone is mild and caring. You may not see them smile frequently and this can come across as stoic and unfriendly. However, this is not always the case.

The great thing about the vast majority of people drawn to this profession is they are good at accomplishing tasks. And there are numerous tasks for which they are responsible. A need for them is to be of service to others. Their job is often a delicate balance of serving the tenants and the property owners, who ultimately pay their bills. They do not like conflict. They also do not like sudden change. When guiding them through tasks, they will need concrete illustrations. It is definitely worth the time to demonstrate this to them because once they get it, they are happy to do it over and over and over again.

In the coming chapter, we will stress the importance of being able to transmit corporate agendas from the top down. This can be an important task for asset managers who are often the go-between for corporate policy and local feet on the ground. If you are very driven and task oriented, slowing down long enough to work with property managers might prove challenging. They can be indecisive, so they will resist making a decision, especially a tough one. So when implementing new policies or agendas, it is important to be warm and personal. Once on board, they will execute tasks like nobody's business. They are absolutely critical to getting things done. Another benefit is their loyalty. Once they are in a good healthy environment, they tend to stick with it.

They like to receive and provide hands-on, personal service; it is of extreme importance to them. One of the biggest helpers in dealing with them successfully is setting them up in an environment in which they can excel. Picture them as complex machinery. It can be difficult to structure it on the front end; however, once it is built it will work as intended without much additional input. Investing time in these relationships can ensure dependable and efficient long-term success.

Vendors

I put this one last because it may be the last skill you really need to develop. Vendors call you. Well, at least their salespeople call you. Salespeople in general will fit into a unique category. I might trash on salespeople a little because I am one. I understand the way most of us think. Most salespeople don't really need a lot from you. And more importantly, you do not need a lot from most salespeople.

Sales is a numbers game. I make literally hundreds of calls to get one client. Not every sales profession is set up this way, but many of them are. Realize that you will not do business with most salespeople that you speak with. And since your time is valuable, you need to deal with them on your terms for your own efficiency's sake.

Before we cover basically how to deal with salespeople, it is much more important for you to learn how to categorize them. Which Quadrant do they fit in? What is the dollar amount of the product that they are selling? How much of this do I need? These questions and others will help you classify the return on time that a relationship with a particular salesperson and their company might provide you. If the return on time is very low, so should be the amount of time you spend with that salesperson. It is critically important that you do not waste time with salespeople that cannot help you very much. But it is much more critical that you not blow off the ones that can!

As with all other relationships, understanding motivations of salespeople is critical; however, they are coming to you, so you have the upper hand in dictating how the relationship goes. If you want to treat them like an ass, they will likely put up with it. I would not say this is the best strategy for you, but learning to sift through salespeople correctly is paramount. If somebody calls to pitch you, give them 30 seconds and an objective ear.

I am mindful of a conversation I had with my boss a few months ago. A salesperson had contacted him about phone service. I don't know what we spend on phone service each month, but I am sure it is quite inexpensive. Therefore, whatever savings this vendor could have provided would certainly have been minimal. He got off the phone quickly because finding the absolute best phone service out there is going to provide very little additional benefit to our company. For some companies, this is a critical component and warrants careful consideration, but for our company it certainly is not. I'm not sure if my boss could have quantified the Return on Time of changing phone systems, but he knew it would have significantly less marginal return than the investment of that time elsewhere in our organization.

So to cover this quickly, people that are drawn to sales as a profession are typically talkative, animated and playful. Because of this, they often annoy the crap out of other people. This is especially true when they are wordy at times they could and should be succinct. They tend to be friendly and like to have fun. Their biggest need is to be accepted and to connect with other people. Contrast this with their biggest fear of being rejected, and you get a person that likes to spend time talking about what others think about them.

To summarize, you are in a position where you deal with many different types of people. Some of these relationships can be quite beneficial and profitable, while others can be a complete waste of time. Learn to prioritize and sort. One of the biggest roles for success in Quadrant A is learning what goes in Quadrants H, T & S.

CHAPTER EIGHT

TRAIN

Quadrant T is certainly the one with the most tasks and assignments. As a result, this chapter will likely have the most practical content. Whereas Quadrant H may lend to you the greatest gains in financial returns, mastering the management of the relationships associated in Quadrant T could see the biggest gains in time management. In the previous chapter we touched on relationships with people that are drawn into property management. We will delve into these a little further, but I want to highlight what was touched on before.

Property managers are doers. They are great at getting things done. It is part of their DNA. Not only are they good at it, it is quite rewarding for them as well. As we stated before, change can be difficult for property managers. They will often resist change. It will take them a while to come around to a new way of thinking. Implementing change with them can be a drawn-out task. But as we stated before, it is a very worthwhile endeavor. Once a new way of thinking is embraced, it will be adhered to.

Recall how we compared implementing changes with building a machine. Machines take time to construct. Tooling them can be quite tedious. Designing and implementing can take hours and hours. The execution may not always go according to plan. Redesigns are quite common. It can be a lengthy process. However, once everything is up and running, the machine is pretty much self-operative. Sure, there may be a little maintenance here and there, but by and large the machine will operate in the manner it is constructed. Consider this as we delve deeper into relationships with property managers.

To start with, property managers are the feet on the ground. They are the liaisons between the public and your corporate product. They have the ability to make or break the operational success of your assets. They not only maintain your corporate image, they *are* your corporate image. It is vitally important that they understand and carry out corporate objectives on a local level.

One problem that topped the list for asset managers was personnel and staffing. It is an enormous challenge to acquire and maintain good people to run your business. Much of the focus from respondents was geared towards finding and keeping good people. ClearFit.com was mentioned as a screening tool that a few respondents used. You can use an outside resource to do a lot of the sifting and screening for you. But more than a timesaver, it is an effective way to match up personnel with the corporate strategy.

Acquiring good people is certainly a challenge. Keeping them around can be as well. Recall in the previous chapters we talked about the importance of job satisfaction for personality types that are drawn to property management. They like to perform tasks in areas that they feel make a difference. Although they are neither highly excitable nor overly friendly, they do like to maintain peaceful relationships with people. They like continuity and agreement and are quite good at bringing it about. They are not great problem solvers, but they are great synthesizers. They use personal care and attention to detail to deliver what some might perceive as bad news. They are warm and fuzzy.

One respondent said that in order to increase job satisfaction of their local people, they decided to close their offices on Sunday. This gave people time off and created a culture that valued the employees' well-being. Another respondent, a multi-family asset manager, said they moved to being closed the entire weekend. This might seem to conflict with being able to provide excellent service to the tenants, however, they deemed the job satisfaction of management as more important, and they were confident that increased satisfaction would have a net positive impact on tenants.

One targeted question we often asked was if throwing money at personnel challenges was a solution. Most people said it was not. The reason why is that most asset managers were talking about staffing people in the service part of their business. In other words, staffing the local feet on the ground. In general, most people that are successful in these roles don't value monetary rewards as much as they value job satisfaction and that feeling they get when they know they're making a difference for their tenants. When you understand this concept, you will be able to attract good people. When you effectively *implement* this concept, you will be able to create and retain good people.

Quadrant T of the HATS Matrix is about training. In baseball, these are obviously the coaches, so a coaching hat is appropriate. Well-coached athletes win baseball games. Well-trained employees provide a good return. So as we further discuss this Quadrant and the relationships associated with it, realize that much of the time spent here is going to be in a coaching, training or mentoring role.

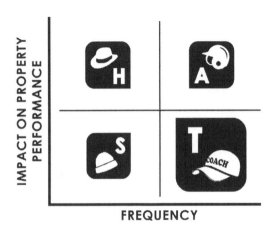

The first challenge in implementing a corporate objective down to a specific property is to realize these local properties will have their own objectives as well. To further complicate things, a third-party property manager will have their own corporate agenda. And their agenda might not be perfectly aligned with yours. In some cases, a replacement might be warranted. But in all cases, communication is certainly warranted.

Before we move on, briefly consider the relationship between the Quadrants and how that scatterplot of tasks looks very different for different roles. For example, working with property managers is primarily in your Quadrant T. However, from the property manager's perspective, many of these same tasks are in *their* Quadrant A. Furthermore, a lot of tasks (or even people) that fall into your Quadrant S will reside in one of their other Quadrants. It's critical as you work with property managers to remember that certain relationships may be far more valuable to them than they are to you. So as you are working with and training them, it is important to understand that these relationships might be more important to others than they are to you.

One respondent had a very strong opinion about how underutilized technology is for many companies. He stressed there are many opportunities available to communicate and carry out corporate objectives through the different levels of the organization. He is likely more tech savvy than most. His biggest criticism is how many companies take an off-the-shelf approach to running their businesses. He stressed how nearly all software packages can be custom-tailored to assist in the management of corporate directives. However, he was amazed at how few people understood this and actually did it. He mentioned how Yardi software could be modified to record and track items specific to any corporate goals with great levels of details. It does require a little customization. But the cost of doing so is totally insignificant compared to the benefits that can be provided.

While he was on his rant, I asked about the cost of implementing this type of customization. I said, "So let me get this straight, a real estate company could spend $5,000 to $10,000 to hire a consultant to implement changes to better serve their hundreds of millions of dollars worth of real estate?" His response was that it would not take anywhere near $5,000. He said in most cases the solution is already been developed for someone else. It is nearly free to implement by simply asking the manufacturer. But even if it did cost $10,000, this is a minimal cost to develop a system to obtain and monitor information on multiple millions of dollars worth of real estate assets.

The application here is that you can track any information you want. If how many Coca-Cola® cans are tossed out in the parking lot is an important statistic for corporate to track, this information can be followed locally and provided centrally. Counting aluminum cans is probably not of high importance. But many statistics are. Technology has created numerous opportunities for us to record and monitor valuable information. In many cases, it is left undone simply for not taking the time to do so.

A different respondent gave a unique perspective. He manages retail and industrial assets for a very large and well-known Dallas-based group. He mentioned how property managers can often err on the side of over-caring. He compared it to the parents of a first-born baby. They go out and buy an $800 stroller and a $500 car seat. This type of mindset might be great if the owner of the property is an insurance company with a 30-year typical hold. But what if the property was bought as a value add? He said we would then be looking for the hand-me-downs that are typically given to a fourth kid.

He stressed that all people involved with a particular asset generally want the same thing – the overall success of the performance of the asset. However, when objectives are not clearly communicated across individuals or organizations, opinions may differ on exactly what this is.

There is a lot of room for frustration when expectations are not met. If a $30,000 chiller is on the fritz, the insurance company might be happy to replace it with a brand spanking new one. The value add guys want to try a roll of duct tape and anything else that will keep it puttering along for another six months. I chuckled when he said that no one goes into a property and makes a buying decision based on how cold the air is. Air conditioning either works or it doesn't. Tenants don't really care if the cold air comes from a brand-new chiller or a 20-year-old one, as long as it's cold.

The takeaway from the conversation with this guy was one thing he wanted to stress. He operated with the following assumption: Everyone wants to be successful. From the top down, from the CEO to the janitor, everyone generally wants to see the success of the asset. However, not everyone sees success in the same manner. Communication and training is key. When people are set up for success, they generally will achieve it. And when they are set up for failure, they will hit that mark as well. He mentioned that it is critical for property managers to think like owners. If this is the case, it is critical to let the property managers know what the owners think.

The Impact of Technology

Technology has certainly created some new challenges and opportunities in the area of property management. We briefly mentioned how it has helped some respondents in their screening process for new employees. Another respondent mentioned how technology has actually enabled them to reduce their number of employees. He had a pretty distinct background in technology. And this background had driven many of his ideas, processes and strategies. Nearly everyone on their staff had smart phones. Their service requests at their properties were done through a smartphone app. This app offered seamless communication from the tenant to the maintenance staff. No paper was ever involved. Rents from tenants were paid online only. Technology was incredibly important to this company, and they required its integration with their employees, vendors and even their tenants.

In leasing, virtual tours have changed the way consumers evaluate space. This can drastically reduce the short list of properties that a prospective tenant is interested in viewing. This can create a lot of opportunities for the owners that offer virtual tours. It can also remove from the short list those that don't. Online service and online payments have eliminated vast amounts of paperwork that were once needed to manage an asset. Reducing paper reduces clutter. This also reduces the amount of people necessary to manage that clutter.

It is important that owners and asset managers understand the impact that technology is having on the real estate environment. On one hand, it is creating great opportunities. On the other hand, it is creating great barriers to entry. As generation X-ers and generation Nexters move into consumer mode, the buying habits of the market changes. Old-school owners with traditional means of doing things are severely limiting their exposure to emerging markets. The old ways simply will not compete and will decrease the demand for products that do not cater to the market's techno tastes.

It is far beyond the scope of this book to cover all of the opportunities and benefits big data and analytics can provide real estate owners. However, it is important to recognize the presence of big data in the real estate environment. Different platforms have emerged and will emerge that offer critical and necessary information. Strategies to accumulate, understand and implement available information will no doubt create advantages to some real estate owners. Analytics for forecasting will enable some to see trends that others won't. These trends seen with analytical tools will lead to wise decisions versus uninformed decisions without them.

Social media has changed the consumer marketplace as a whole. What started off as a simple way to exchange vacation photos and baby pics has become a virtual bitch-and-moan platform for politics, religion and the marketplace in general. Twenty years ago a virtual footprint might be something left in an area near a Bigfoot sighting (then again it might not!?). Today, anyone and everything has some sort of online reputation to manage. This can be great and awful at the same time.

Websites, blogs, Facebook, Twitter and other social media have created numerous outlets for people to express both praise and disdain. Companies, officers, employees and assets can all have their own social media reputations to manage. When managed properly, these can be great selling tools. When managed improperly, they can be of great harm. A property can have a Facebook page that can serve as a virtual advertisement to the outside world. It can also be a place were disgruntled tenants voice their frustration to the public. This will attract all sorts of comments including the good, the bad and the ugly. One insightful strategy was offered to get around this: A respondent suggested creating an internal Facebook group for tenants or residents of a particular asset. This would be a way, although not a foolproof way, to keep some negative comments "within the family." This is a very good idea.

Some study somewhere suggested that buying habits were more often influenced by someone else's comment than any other cause. In other words, I don't want to look up the source. But it sounds pretty good. The idea behind this is a referral or a testimonial. As consumers, we are all influenced by the buying decisions of others. An endorsement goes a long way. An endorsement from someone we trust goes even farther. A good virtual reputation can drive business to you. A bad virtual reputation will do just the opposite. For this reason, it is very important to remedy negative feedback and comments at all costs.

In general, people that go to the trouble to voice frustration do often have legitimate complaints. Sure, every once in a while you may have some crackpot just blowing off steam. But by and large, people that post feedback have taken the trouble to do so for a reason. This alone gives some level of credibility to their comments. If negative feedback is given about one of your assets, it can certainly be detrimental. However, it can also be an opportunity.

There is a martial art that uses the energy and momentum of your opponent to your advantage. It is called Aikido. I'm pretty sure there are other labels for similar art forms, but I believe this is the main one. If your opponent comes at you too hard, you can step out of his way and push him on his face. Or if he tries to punch you, then you can redirect his thumb towards his eyeball. You get the idea. You can redirect his own aggression and energy towards him to your advantage.

There is a similar practice in business that I like to call Disgruntled Client Aikido. This can be used in a situation where a client has an unpleasant experience, and you use this negative energy and redirect it for a positive outcome.

Technology has given people a new platform for voicing frustration that did not exist much more than a decade ago. People can vent, and their voice will be heard or read. This is great until you or your company or your company's asset becomes the target of their frustration. If you find yourself on the receiving end of this, the good news is that this negativity can be redirected. I have found that some very mad customers can become quite vocal. I have also found that when dealt with properly, these energized and vocal disgruntled customers can be turned into the most vocal, happy customers when their needs get met. Negative comments can be great opportunities.

A ticked off customer has more energy than a neutral one. People who are indifferent rarely go to the trouble to complain. People who are mad often do. Others who read reports of disgruntled complaints are sensational for most and often relatable. The best outcome for one of these complaints is a follow up post where the same person addresses the solution in addition to the complaint. Everyone experiences problems, but not everyone has those problems solved for them. When you go to the trouble to repair the social media breaches about your company and assets, it tells the market that you are a problem solver. This negative energy and experience can be turned into a positive one. People who complain well are often the ones that will praise well too. Other people in the marketplace can relate to both the frustrations and the solutions very well.

Managing social media is becoming a critical function for many businesses. Larger companies may find it beneficial to centralize this process with a person or even staff devoted to monitoring the company's image in the virtual world. With many individual assets, this can become quite a large undertaking. It also must be done in conjunction with local management, as client complaints are generally specific to local issues and done on a local level. Regardless of the strategy you use to monitor your reputation, it is very important to ensure that all issues are discovered and addressed. It is also critical that these roles and functions be coached properly with the right training for the responsible parties.

There are also services that can help manage this process. They can gather information from numerous social media sites and compile it for you. This frees you and your staff from hunting and gathering content about your company and assets by bringing it to you. No one has the time to scour every possible outlet of potential complaints from customers. It is much more effective to have this done for you. When managing your online reputation, it is important that corporate tactics and strategies are carried out at all levels of the organization.

Quadrant T is dependent on your overall ability to coach and train others effectively. On a sports team, coaches exist to bring the players to their highest and best use and to get them to play to their full potential. The goal of coaching, therefore, should be to optimize the performance of the team. This skill can be greatly hindered by someone who likes to take on everything themselves. An effective coach is much more concerned about his player's performance than his own recognition. The average efforts of a group of people will always outperform the best efforts of one. Consider then how much greater the performance will be of those who are well coached and driven to be excellent.

Coaching individuals or groups begins with effective communication. It is absolutely essential that all members of the team know the expectations and goals of the organization. After communication comes buy-in. Success is dependent on all members of the team understanding and being a part of the organizational goals. Generally speaking, this buy-in will take place in one of two forms. It can happen by relationship, where the corporate vision is accepted because it is carefully delivered and willingly accepted by choice. It can also happen by force. When resistance is encountered in the area of management, positional authority will often demand adherence to corporate objectives. Once participants understand and accept the company goals, they can be implemented. Once properly set into motion, this can become a well-oiled machine.

Effective coaching can result in large teams of people effectively carrying out the company goals. A good coach can manage large teams of people. Teams of people can always get more done than individuals ever could. Leverage is essential in Quadrant T. Effective asset management is directly tied to managing teams effectively.

As stated above, this can be done by relationship or by force. I personally find that it is more powerful and effective to make people *want* to do something than to make them actually do it. When people are motivated by force, the motivation required to accomplish the task goes away once the force is removed.

Dwight D. Eisenhower was the Supreme Commander of the Allied Forces in Europe during World War II. His leadership was instrumental in defeating the Nazis and the Axis powers. He later became the 34th president of the United States. He had the following to say about leadership styles:

"Persuasion is always the best form of leadership. Instead of having your followers think that they're just doing what they're told, persuasion implies ownership. They follow you because they want to, not because they have to."

— Dwight D. Eisenhower

When people desire to carry out objectives, the motivation is internal and constant. Contrast this style with tyrants who lead by intimidation and fear. When people follow orders out of fear, once the force is removed so is the motivation to follow the desires of the leader.

In the case of Eisenhower, his foe in WWII was a militaristic tyrant who dreadfully led Germany by extreme measure of force. Hitler survived more than one assassination attempt by his subordinates and ultimately ended his own life. When force is used to steer people, they may or may not agree with your goals. If they do not agree with your objectives, they often will attempt to carry out their own.

When addressing tasks that fall in the high-frequency and low-cost of Quadrant T, a great team and effective training are essential. Healthy functioning teams create leverage, which greatly multiplies an asset manager's Return on Time and the return on energy expended.

If you have any amount of kids to go home to, then the concept of return on energy expended needs to be super high! Better take as much home with you on a daily basis as you can find. Well-trained teams can help with this greatly.

Think of the silly acronym for TEAM: Together Everyone Achieves More. How about this one: **T**raining = **E**lated **A**sset **M**anager. In the next chapter, we will address the final Quadrant of the HATS Matrix.

CHAPTER NINE

SCRAP

Now let's move on to Quadrant IV, aka Quadrant S. We have spent a lot of time trashing this Quadrant and minimizing its value. It is good to not give items in this Quadrant too much time. However, if it were completely worthless to investigate, we would not devote an entire chapter of *Pain in the Asset Manager* to it. We would simply make it a footnote and then move on.

In our baseball organization, the Scrap crew are the ones cleaning up the stadium after the games. The work here is not very consistent. It is seasonal and event driven. It is generally extra work for those who do it and not a complete source of income for them. It might compliment other things that they do, but it will not stand alone for the sake of stability.

What is critical about this Quadrant and the one above it, Quadrant H, is knowing how to categorize and sort what goes in them.

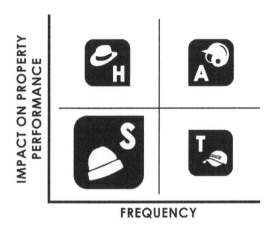

Actually, this sorting is important to all of the Quadrants of the HATS Matrix, but dealing with items in the Quadrants on the left side of the HATS Matrix typically includes the vendors associated with them. Salespeople can often rub us the wrong way. This often causes us to limit the amount of time spent dealing with them. I am not suggesting that we all develop better listening skills and give them all the time of day. I do think it is wise, though, to not let any aversion to them cause you to do a poor job of sorting and evaluating the additional benefit one might bring to you.

Years ago I worked as an insurance consultant in commercial construction. We identified claims that could be filed with insurance companies that could be pursued to restore properties to pre-loss conditions. In the area that we worked, roofs were often damaged unaware to the owners. When brought to their attention, they had an opportunity to pursue a claim. This awareness started with a visual inspection of the property.

One property that I successfully moved from potential to realistic claim was with the CFO of a specialty manufacturer. His name was Danny. He had been called dozens of times by numerous vendors about this same issue. He had also tried twice in the past unsuccessfully to produce the outcome I was waving in front of him. Even though he had dealt with this more than once in the past without result and heard from scores of others offering the same, he listened. He listened long enough to be convinced that he should again open up this case for investigation. The end result was that Danny qualified for a claim, and he received several hundred thousand dollars for restoration.

What Danny did in this example was sort properly. He successfully reclassified a routinely placed roofing contractor (Quadrant S) into a consultant (Quadrant H) for navigating through the cumbersome insurance claims arena. He took something infrequent and of low potential value (roof maintenance) and repositioned it as infrequent with high-potential value. The ability to sort through this quickly produced an opportunity that he had attempted and overlooked in the past.

To dissect even further, a roofing contractor would likely not be an extremely valuable relationship for an asset manager. What typically puts them in Quadrant S is that roofs are replaced very infrequently, although maintained on a more periodic basis. The value that one roofer can create over another is not typically that great. The performance and quality is often a big differentiator, but the amount of money spent over a 10-to-20-year period on roofing is not going to change an awful lot by investigating this type of service. That is why until further notice, they should be classified in Quadrant S.

142

In Danny's example, he temporarily suspended his opinion of low-frequency occurrence and *low* value to low-frequency of occurrence and *high* value. He later told me he thought in his head, I will give this guy 30 seconds and listen to what he has to say. In that time, I convinced him to consider things from a different viewpoint. What I actually did was compare the value risked, a couple of minutes on the phone, with the potential payout of a restored roof to the building. The value of the claim topped $800,000. Not bad for a couple of minutes on the phone. He moved me from the Scrap Quadrant S to the Hire Quadrant H, and he did not waste much time in doing so. His evaluation of the product offering then had the appropriate risk/reward values assigned to it. This enabled the decision to be discussed and measured properly.

Your time as an asset manager is very valuable. You are responsible for millions, tens of millions or even hundreds of millions of dollars in real estate assets. You cannot take calls from every single vendor; to do so would be unreasonable and would consume all of your time. You can prioritize and shift things when the potential impact justifies it. You must know when to do this. As soon as Danny's claim was handled, roof maintenance and insurance claims quickly moved back from Quadrant H to Quadrant S. Until another event causes a potential claim, roofing contractors are not going to provide him a very high Return on Time.

Lots of products and services fit into the Scrap Quadrant S for asset managers. Topping the list are the services and supplies that are needed on a local level or per-asset basis. The reason the time spent on these should be minimized is the potential value that an improvement in one of these areas can make is pretty minimal. Buying the best and most economical janitorial supplies might provide some other great benefit to you, but a shift in profitability is not one of them. This holds true for nearly all items that are purchased infrequently and do not cost a lot of money.

We have drilled home the concept that Quadrant S is not a good place for an asset manager to invest much time. This may not hold true for property managers. Because property managers focus often on a single asset or smaller group of assets, they will have a more hands-on understanding of how these more local vendor relationships can be optimized. Furthermore, some of the line items might weigh in higher in a property manager's HATS Matrix. Your training of them should place some of your Quadrant S items in their Quadrants H, A or T.

Some efficiencies may exist for consolidating services with local vendors. A landscape contractor might offer a discount to you for servicing several properties instead of just one. This is a decent area of focus for property managers, but not likely asset managers. How much bottom-line impact would this savings really have? It is likely not that great and not a great area for you to increase your Return on Time. Property managers should be encouraged to evaluate these individual vendors in relation to their own personal Return on Time. What could be perceived as low-margin for you, might actually be a high impact item for them.

The attitude one should take in dealing with Quadrant S is not complete dismissal. There are opportunities here, but they are limited and not greatly significant. Remember the story of Cliff? The farmer he hired out found some gold at times, but it was never in great quantities; it did have value to him, but not enough to cause a major shift. One respondent mentioned the following tactic for increasing return to investors and the impact on property values. He mentioned paint of all things. He knew that if he could trim $3/gallon off of the paint that they used for multi-family make readies, it would add $5,000 annually to NOI. He then connected the dots for the value of the property at a 5% CAP would add $100,000 to the sales price.

This particular respondent was pretty high up in his company. He was a bit unique in the industry because his background was property management, and he had risen pretty high up in an asset management role. Due to his background, he would see opportunities that others didn't. He also gives us a great opportunity to show the relationships of these Quadrants.

One of the best ways to distinguish what is on your plate and what should be on your property manager's plate is by looking at purchasing power. Who can most effectively take your demand for certain products or services to the market and shop it accordingly? Property managers likely have buying power on tangible commodities like those listed, since they tend to manage multiple properties in a given geographic area. Air filters, coffee and snacks, cleaning supplies, and office supplies make little to no sense to consolidate on a corporate level. These might make sense in a region with several assets within close proximity to one another. As we have mentioned in the Hire chapter, consolidating insurance or energy demand can create significant savings and should be handled on a regional or corporate level.

Recall that we mentioned that some of the things in your Quadrant S might be a property manager's Quadrant H, A or T. In other words, they might spend time on something that would not make a lot of sense for you to spend time on. Because of this, they may uncover an opportunity that would go unnoticed to you. When this happens, the first questions you should consider is: Can this be replicated in other assets or regions? Technology is rapidly evolving. Opportunities are popping up for efficiency everywhere. When a good one comes along, measure the impact of implementing these across the board.

Low impact items should generally stay in the low Quadrants. But they will shift at times. Temporary changes can cause great alterations to the placement of a task within the HATS Matrix. For instance, your GC who handles finish out improvements is a low-impact vendor for the most part. You may spend a lot of money with him, but the service is generally replaceable, and the cost is not going to vary greatly from one supplier to the next. However, a fire or other casualty might move this routine vendor into a specialized category that places him in a different Quadrant. The frequency may not change much, but the change in impact could be huge. Consider the impact of a one-day delay. This could be insignificant with a single new tenant moving in, but with numerous tenants in temporary space due to a casualty loss, it's a game changer.

The sweeping generalization here is when issues have a high impact on income or *could* have a high impact, it is wise to get involved. It is also important not to task local managers with items that generally fall in the high-impact Quadrants. It is not because they are incapable of dealing with high-value transactions. It is more because the less frequent and high-impact items can create opportunities or challenges that lower-impact items generally do not. They should be treated differently.

The hiring parameters are not the same for Property Maintenance Management and Property Tax Management. If Property Maintenance messes up, it is immediately recognizable and easy to address. If Property Tax people mess up, it may take nearly a year to uncover their mistakes and become hard to know when it is best to actually cut bait. Additionally, think about the range of cost to you in hiring the absolute worst maintenance company versus the absolute best. Once the poor hiring decision becomes evident, they could be replaced and getting the best vendor in there might take three or four months. Any financial loss due to the worst possible maintenance management company should be relatively easy to recover from.

Now consider comparing hiring the absolute worst Property Tax consultant with hiring the absolute best. The range of performance is a 0% percentage increase to a 15% to 20% or even more in the same markets. The impact of this is hundreds of thousands of dollars, and the time to evaluate and replace them takes at least a year. The financial problems due to poor performance could take a significant amount of time to recover from.

We encountered very few asset managers or owners that left these types of high impact decisions in the hands of property managers, but it does happen. The cost of doing this can be great, and it is generally a bad practice. We have listed other reasons previously, but recall the general temperament traits of people drawn into property management. They do not like to make big decisions, and they do not like change. This is not characteristic of someone who will assertively make a needed hiring decision because of a performance problem.

An asset manager that understands the concept of Return on Time and applies the sifting concept of the HATS Matrix will maximize their own efficiency and returns on each asset.

Spending too much time in Quadrant S can be labeled as "majoring in the minors." This Quadrant cannot be completely ignored, but it should be minimized. For the asset manager, these items should be delegated to others in the organization unless their impact changes or purchasing patterns can change the significance that they have. Regardless, this attention should be limited because it is short term and will not require ongoing maintenance. I would liken it to sending in a pinch-hitter. It is a temporary suspension of normal operations until normal patterns can be returned to. And this should be done quickly.

Before we close, I also want to reiterate the importance of categorizing vendors correctly. Some belong in Quadrant H and some belong in Quadrant S. Even if you dislike salespeople, you're going to have to stomach the fact that some of them are a necessary evil. If you categorize energy and tax consultants in the same category as coffee and copy machine salespeople, you are overlooking the impact that each of them could potentially provide you and your company.

Also, invest a little bit of time in hearing a different approach to meeting your current needs — even if you currently have what you consider to be a great service provider. Be willing to give someone half a minute to convey to you the reason that they called. A seasoned salesperson should be able to succinctly communicate to you a small handful of key differentiators for you to consider. They should be able to do this quickly. If their elevator pitch fails to intrigue you, then feel free to move on. But before you dismiss them completely, consider that the greatest hindrance to opening a doorway of opportunity is a closed mind.

"Being ignorant is not so much a shame, as being unwilling to learn."

— Ben Franklin

CHAPTER TEN

THE GRAND SLAM

As we wrap up *Pain in the Asset Manager*, I want to lay the groundwork for what is next. If you have made it this far, I would like to continue to push you in the same direction. There are several great concepts in this book. The problem is that they can help you a lot or not at all. The greatest warm thoughts and head nods about these concepts will produce absolutely nothing for you. However, acting on them will.

I want to encourage you to take the ideas and suggestions here and bring them into your professional environment. I want to challenge you to swing for the fences with the following Grand Slam strategy that begins with the Big Three.

Throughout this book we have discussed skills, tactics and strategies that your peers have claimed are beneficial to them in their asset management careers. We have compiled these, sorted them, and are now presenting them in what we believe is a straightforward manner. In maintaining the focus of our book, our goal is to give you the small list of causes that will generate the large list of results.

In Chapter 3, we mentioned the Big Three and the Grand Slam. These are labels we placed on a few key areas of focus that we believe will have the greatest impact on your performance as an asset manager. In our program, the Big Three is one part of the bigger Grand Slam.

We introduced it because the items in it were already familiar to everyone, although the strategies and tactics might not have been. The remaining parts to the Grand Slam will be introduced after a very quick review of the Big Three.

The Big Three

The Big Three was presented earlier as a handful of things to implement that would greatly increase the bottom-line return to investors. We strongly believe that this is the best place for you to start because it is in line with the Pareto Principle. We pointed out how small rudders turn big ships.

Small tools or concepts that are properly employed can greatly alter the course of direction. Once anyone would accept the concept of Return on Time, we would suggest spending enough time to implement these changes within your assets or organization.

1. Federal Tax Management
2. Property Tax Management
3. Energy Cost Management

The Federal Tax savings opportunities can most often generate the largest initial returns to investors. Because the savings do not fall within an asset's net operating income, these opportunities are not often addressed by asset managers, if at all. However, once implemented, they will probably have the greatest initial impact over any of the other suggestions in this book. They do not affect pre-tax earnings, but they greatly impact the post-tax earnings and most importantly, the return to investors.

As previously mentioned, the best property tax management results seem to be created with a comprehensive, soup to nuts property tax strategy. The strategy involves a coordinated "CAD to Courtroom" effort with a team of seasoned and knowledgeable professionals who work well together. Additionally, we mentioned that the best way to evaluate your tax provider is to compare his result with the market. Most tax professionals are happy to compare the end result with the starting point. These numbers will always show that you are receiving some value, but they can often be skewed to paint whatever picture is attractive at the time. Comparing your end result with other like properties in the same market will give you a much better representation of their performance. Remember, this result will only be favorable for about 35% to 40% of consultants. The rest of them will range from just above to far below average.

Energy Cost Management is another leg of the Big Three. This is something that should be monitored on a periodic basis. If your method of addressing this has been to sign agreements and wait for them to expire, you are missing great opportunities to take advantage of market fluctuations. This is especially true if your timing ranges from peak to peak. Working with an energy consultant who is constantly mindful of savings opportunities for you is indicated by them being in contact with you on a periodic basis. Great opportunities exist in deregulated states, especially when you combine purchasing power across a number of assets.

Anyone who has not given great attention to all of the elements of the Big Three could certainly benefit by focusing on more of them. Because the Return on Time is greatest in these high-impact areas, we suggest this as a starting point for improving asset performance. Most of the respondents surveyed admitted that they do not incorporate all of these measures and very few gave more than one of them their attention.

If you fit into this category, this is really good news. It is good news because the coming changes in the real estate market will require creativity to set yourself apart. Normal business operations will likely cease to generate above normal returns. The expectation in the market is for this to happen sooner rather than later. No one has perfect information, but a time is coming when maintaining the status quo will not produce the same results that it has in past years. To stand out and lead the pack, you will need to look for money in other places. Remember, there is gold in the side of the mountain!

Sort with the HATS Matrix

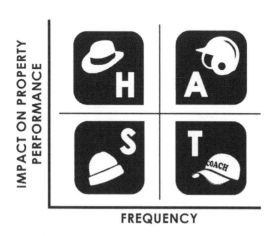

FREQUENCY

We first want to challenge you to utilize the concept in the HATS Matrix for sorting and prioritizing your day-to-day activities. The concept of Return on Time could revolutionize the way you spend your day. Urgent and pressing needs are not always the most valuable and seldom the most beneficial recipients of your efforts and time. Urgent activities may be a pressing need for someone else to address. It might often be your job or duty to determine who this person is. When you develop an efficient system for processing all of these activities, then the tasks that come your way can be delegated to the appropriate person in the position of each Quadrant.

Keep in mind that maintaining the relationships with people in each of these Quadrants is a Quadrant A activity for you; however, the duties and activities that they focus on are not. When you put effective people and tools in place, it is not necessary to micromanage their job functions. Their tasks are simply that, *their tasks.* You need to make sure that you allow them the freedom and flexibility to perform the duties that you have hired them to do. If this is difficult for you, you need to develop your skill of empowering others. Recall what was said about the leadership styles of Eisenhower versus Hitler. One eventually became a delusional, suicidal statistic. The other eventually became an iconic president.

When employing others, your responsibility goes from doing their jobs to gathering the necessary information about the jobs that they are doing. Most of this they should provide to you. But some of it you will have to gather on your own. It is in our nature to put forth good information when we are evaluating ourselves. Although this information can often be true, it is not always complete. As an effective manager of other people's assets, it is important that you do not rely solely on people's self-evaluations.

Never become complacent as a consumer based on your relationship with the supplier. Always realize there is a chance that someone else out there could possibly do a better job or provide a better service. I often hear the phrase, "I've been working with Joe Blow, and he has been doing this for me for 25 years!" The first question I like to ask when I hear this is, "Well, is he any good at it?" The answers generally fit into one of two categories. The first category is a pretty confident "yes," followed by a rather knowledgeable explanation of the work that is done. I have this type of relationship with a friend who handles most of my personal insurance needs. For the last 18 years he has consistently kept me shopping the market to ensure I fall in the bottom 10% to 20% of premiums that I could pay. More often than not, though, the answer to the "doing a good job question" fits into this second category. They seem to take offense at the question about being good at it, often because they honestly don't know. In this case, the relationship might be worth more than the value lost due to poor performance.

Most of your relational management will be spent on people within Quadrant H or Quadrant T. Remember, people that fall in your Quadrant S will fall in someone else's Quadrant H, A or T. Let them maintain that relationship. You should not often deal with people in Quadrant S, unless they provide a temporary shift into your Quadrant H. Here is an example: A few years ago, I heard a sales pitch from a guy who had a patent on a water-saving device. He claimed that this device when attached to a water meter would compress the air molecules in the water line. This would actually shrink the volume of any air going through the water meter, causing the water bill to be less — up to 30% less.

Honestly, I do not think this product worked as claimed. They could actually prove that air bubbles in the line would shrink greatly, almost totally, while passing through their device. What they didn't prove and probably cannot prove is the existence of a significant amount of air in people's waterlines. If the claims could be substantiated, this would move a Quadrant S plumbing salesperson into a Quadrant H water efficiency vendor who could have a much greater bottom-line impact. However, as stated before, this would be a temporary shift until the product was evaluated and purchased or, ultimately, decided against.

The important takeaway here is not how much money you might be able to save with innovative plumbing products or any other type of product for that matter. What is important is classifying roles and relationships in a manner that enables you to maximize your Return on Time.

Train Your Team

One of the best things you can do for your sanity is to invest time in managing your managers. This was discussed in greater detail in the Training chapter on activities that fall within your Quadrant T. Proper training in this arena will create a team that is able and willing to execute company directives with little input. Remember how we compared it to building a machine. People drawn to property management generally like routines and execution of tasks. They do not like confrontation, challenges or change. This really is the perfect description of people who enjoy stable environments.

Remember how it was reported that throwing money at this type of personnel may not be the best way to ensure that someone is content in their position and in line with the corporate mindset? Proper screening and training does ensure just that. As you train local level managers and employees, remember that they need to feel like they are making a difference for job satisfaction. They do not need excessive amounts of money and will not often ask for it. This is not to discourage rewarding them financially, but do not expect doing so to correct behavior or align them to objectives they weren't aligned with previously.

Recall the importance of pushing corporate goals through regions and local teams. This can be quite challenging and requires time and the right strategy. Very few people genuinely like change. Most of us dislike it at best, and we tend to resist it. This is especially true for people — many people — who are drawn to property management. When implementing changes, it is important to not make changes frequently. This is extremely frustrating for them. If you will do the job of implementing change effectively and infrequently, you'll find they will support it and will be the ones to enforce it effectively once set in motion.

Technology can be enhanced and specialized to assist in conveying and monitoring company values through the flow of information. Spending time on technological implementation can greatly enhance efficiency and even job satisfaction for many.

A number of companies when bringing about technological change will talk about it up front but fail to see it through the implementation phase. This frustrates people who do not like change to begin with. One thing worse than change is the introduction of coming changes that are not fully seen through to the end.

Do not forget the importance of hand-holding as changes are made. You may spend an inordinate amount of time on training and implementation. Just remember that the end result can be people working for you who will effectively execute concepts and job assignments repeatedly as desired. They enjoy what is familiar and do not desire challenges or adding excitement to their routine. If they are coddled and encouraged, then they will be the ones who will provide excellent client service in a very stable environment.

Motivate Yourself and Others

Never forget the power of motivation. Whatever motivates, motivates. It goes without saying: Motivated people do not need to be told why to do things. This takes care of itself. They do it because they are motivated to do it. They may need direction in what to do, but they will find the proper reason to do it.

We addressed, in general terms, how most of the professional groups that you will deal with will have similarities in their motivational preferences and the way they communicate. If you want to make great enhancements to your professional relationships, then learn more — much more — about different temperaments and how to better communicate with them. This is a great and often overlooked skill. We spend years in school learning to improve language skills, math skills, writing skills and computer skills. But very little time is required of students on ANY level to improve their people skills. Every source of revenue that we seek in any business or client relationship has a person on the other end with a checkbook. People are who make buying decisions, not books, calculators, budgets or computers. People spend money. If we want to increase our earnings, we better understand the people that will help improve them.

Do yourself a favor — learn what motivates you. If you want to be better at your job, have a reason for working that continues to exist after you leave the office. Take the time to get to know what you enjoy and make sure your current work environment is a good fit for you and your motivations. There is nothing worse than working for someone or a company that is not rewarding for you. If you find yourself in a less than spectacular environment, put a plan together to get out of it. And plan ahead. If you do this on your terms, it will likely produce a much more favorable outcome.

If your fulfillment at work is low, then it will be difficult for you to help enhance other people's fulfillment. In the same way, once you learn how to identify and satisfy your own motivations, it will be easier for you to do the same for other people. If your fulfillment at work is high, then it will be easier for you to help enhance other people's fulfillment. Imagine being the motivational force at work that other people come to for encouragement.

This skill is so simple to learn, and it is not hard at all to develop and implement. This is especially true for people who are friendly. But even if you are selfish and stingy, you can learn it the same. If you need a selfish reason to do it, it will make you more money. It will also increase your influence. By increasing your people skills, you will actually have more people in your sphere of influence with whom to be selfish and stingy. Of course, you might actually become *un*selfish and not stingy in the process. It could actually change the way you relate to people.

The force behind this is a simple word called "honor." This is not a new concept. It has been written about many times before. One of my favorite books written about this is Dale Carnegie's *How to Win Friends and Influence People*. The gist of this book is simple. People want to feel special and important. If you help others do this, they in turn will want to do it for you. Help others get what they want, and they will help you get what you want.

For most of us, human nature is quite simple. The vast majority of us will respond to and are motivated by this type of honor. Sure, there are some sadistic, evil, hell-bent people out there. But they are the exception, not the norm. They also will respond to this type of honor. It might just take a little longer, lowering your Return on Time (Ha-Ha)! But by and large, this is a very useful skill set to develop. As mentioned many times before, it works in *all* relationships, not just business relationships.

Can't get your teenager to clean his room? Recall the mother who thought her teenager was completely unmotivated. He was, however, very motivated to play video games. When she learned to honor his motivation, she could then begin to express her own. Once this mutual honor is expressed, it is easier to put a solution in place. I have seen this in my own 12-year-old. He loves video games, computer time or any type of screen time. Sometimes, this seems completely counterproductive as it relates to getting his homework done. Given the option, he would choose 100% screen time and no school time. The solution is not 0% screen time. The solution is a reward structure where the focus is on his motivation. He can be rewarded with screen time for successful completion of schoolwork, or any other activity that we, as his parents, are motivated for him to complete.

This simple strategy can work in the most complex relationships. Anyone can stomach a little pain. Most of us, however, will try to avoid a lot of pain. Since change often brings about some level of discomfort, it is important to present it in a way where it is minimized. Focusing on a lot of change can consume people; however, focusing on the benefits of working through a little bit of struggle can often make sense to the staunchest of opponents.

THE

GRAND
SLAM

Hit the BIG THREE.

Sort Using the HATS Matrix.

Train your Team.

Motivate Yourself and Others.

So to recap: Swing, Sort, Train and Motivate. These additional focal points, in conjunction with your current skill set, will vastly increase your effectiveness, efficiency and satisfaction at work. You can actually accomplish more by doing less. You can increase your Return on Time. You do this by focusing on what matters most and minimizing what does not.

Pareto came across an interesting discovery when he observed that most results are generated from just a few causes. Remember when we were growing up as kids the commercial that said, "Four out of five dentists recommend blah, blah, blah for their patients who chew gum." In their words, most dentists recommend our gum. However, this means that 1 out of 5 did not. Their focus was that 4 out of 5 did, dismissing the other with the assumption that this guy was an idiot because he did not endorse the gum. I believe he is a difference maker because he realizes that he is a dentist and not a gum shill.

Truthfully, what does chewing gum have to do with healthy teeth? Not a lot.

The one lone dentist proves the Pareto Principle. You know this dental survey was geared to generate an answer that only a "moron" would actually not recommend whatever the product is. This one lone dentist would have to sift through the question that only gives two options. If your patient chews gum, would you recommend this one loaded with sugar and tooth destroying micro-bots or our brand? I bet he had to take quite a stand against what everyone else was doing. "I am not going to recommend your gum or any other for that matter. I choose the non-existent option three! No chewing gum cleans teeth! I may look like an idiot, but the bigger idiots are falling into your corporate strategy to skew the survey. I'm a dentist. My bigger agenda is actual dental care for patients, not selling gum." This dentist will actually have a positive impact on dental care. He is the one standout that promotes dental health over pushing some corporate product for the sake of ease, convenience or getting through some stupid survey.

The point here is not to ditch the status quo and be some non-conventional renegade for the sake of being different. All dentists focus on the same goal most of the time, which is dental health. Being effective does not mean that you shift your focus away from what everyone else is doing, but do not focus *solely* on what everyone else is doing. For the dentists, chewing gum sales are not their livelihood. Promoting gum is a Quadrant S activity that really should be avoided. What the lone dentist really knew is that endorsing gum as a means to dental health would have an overall negative effect if it was promoted as a substitute for what actually does work.

Pareto's philosophy applies to many things. It might apply to *everything*. From my observation, it certainly applies to real estate asset management. If this is so, then 80% of the success in asset management is created by 20% of asset managers. I can hear the commercial now, "Four out of five asset managers maintain the status quo for investors who choose real estate." This means that only one in five will step outside the box and act on opportunities that will actually generate exceptional results. Which one are you?

ABOUT THE AUTHORS

Tim Nichols has always been drawn to creativity, efficiency and innovation. He has spent the better part of his professional career in B2B sales and consulting within the commercial real estate industry. Upon graduating from Texas A&M University with a BBA in Finance and Accounting, he was drawn to a career in real estate that began as an office and industrial tenant-rep broker in Dallas, Texas. Eventually his creative pursuits led him to branch out into additional areas of deal structuring and sourcing for various types of real estate investors. During 2006 and 2007, he worked with a handful of West Coast investors who were interested in acquiring properties and investments in North Texas structured as Tenant in Common investments. In 2008, he decided to go out on his own as a Commercial Real Estate Broker. History has proven this move to be poorly timed. Needless to say, additional means of income became necessary for a few years.

His experience in real estate has given him an ability to navigate through investment offices and corporate structures to locate and address those responsible for asset management functions within their organizations. He has an uncanny talent for addressing these asset managers in a manner that makes his product or service relevant to the hearer, and he can quickly and succinctly present a value proposition to the listener. Tim's desire for innovation and efficiency has caused him to seek out and offer services with a high potential impact for a relatively nominal investment of time and resources.

Currently, Tim works as the Vice President of Business Development for Pinnacle Property Group, a full-service

Property Tax Consulting and Litigation firm based out of Fort Worth, Texas. His extensive marketing of their services led to the compilation of ideas and research that has gone into this publication of *Pain in the Asset Manager*. In combined efforts with co-author Jonathan Gilstrap, the two have compiled hundreds of hours of investigative research in a clear and unique manner. The goal of their research was to identify and understand high-return areas of focus and strategies of addressing them that will create above-normal returns for time invested.

Jonathan Gilstrap earned his BBA in Finance and Risk Management from University of North Texas. He received his MBA from Texas Christian University with a focus on Marketing and Supply Chain. He has over 10 years experience as a business consultant, which began with his financial statement modeling and analysis of investment opportunities. Prior to entering a career in real estate investing and consulting as a Principal of Pinnacle Property Group, he assisted Lockheed Martin in developing a process to evaluate their ROI on Leadership Development Programs. This gave him a keen insight to developing strategies that would both enhance the performance of high-level employees and the associated profitability margins.

Jonathan's analytical capacity is a great complement to his co-author's out-of-the-box thinking. The two play well together. One's tendency to stay grounded paired with the other's desire to aim for the clouds creates a stable flight plan that delivers both creative and attainable solutions. *Pain in the Asset Manager* is the overflow of these well-balanced qualities paired with information obtained from extensive research and investigation.

ORDERING

Email Orders: info@pinnaclepg.com

Fax Orders: 817-570-7091

Telephone Orders: Toll Free: 855-570-9990

Postal Orders:
Pinnacle Property Group, 3617 Hulen St.,
Fort Worth, TX 76107. USA, 817-570-9990

☐ Please send _____ copies of *Pain in the Asset Manager*. Cost is **$19.95** per copy. Please call for bulk pricing on 10 or more copies.

☐ Check
☐ AMEX ☐ Discover ☐ VISA ☐ MasterCard

NAME

ADDRESS

TELEPHONE   EMAIL

CITY   ST   ZIP CODE

CREDIT CARD NO

NAME AS IT APPEARS ON CARD

EXPIRATION DATE   CVC CODE   SIGNATURE

Sales Tax: Please add 8.25% for books shipped to Texas addresses.

www.painintheassetmanager.com
www.pinnaclepg.com

Made in the USA
San Bernardino, CA
29 February 2020